I0541733

inwords

rigo garcia jr.

Crows Press Publishing
Hayward, California

inwords © 2024 by Rigo Garcia Jr.
First Printing, 2024
All rights reserved. Printed in the United States of America.

This book or any portion thereof may not be reproduced or used in any manner whatsoever without the express written permission of the publisher except for the use of brief quotations in a book review.

Self-Published by Rigo Garcia Jr. 6" x 8" (15.24 x 20.32 cm) Black & White on White paper. 248 pages. ISBN: 979-8-218-50260-7

Cover Art, Book Design, & Illustrations all done by Rigo Garcia Jr.

BISAC: Poetry / American / General

contact: rigo.garcia.jnr@gmail.com

for the loners

contents

i. personal history   **1**

Wings or Cages...2

Portal...4

Ethereal...6

Home...8

Not Long After 10

Spit & Bones..12

2 break uh promise 14

Burnt Carpet..16

I've...18

No Role Models...20

I Remember...22

Your Convenience 24

rorriM..26

It Could Have Been 28

The Kitchen Lights..30

Gavel..32

Mirage..34

Deadication..36

ii. here nor there   **39**

Fragmented..40

Dissolve...42

Compost...44

Your Surface World...46

I Am Frail 48

Colors...50

Hold..52

Domestic Silence 54

Parallel...56

Nothing Feels Real 58

Worlds' Away...60

i Think i Was 8...62

I was 4teen...64

Ancestors 66

Words They Say...68

Neither Here Nor There 70

iii. the infinite   **73**

Crows (to my pops) 74

Lunar Eclipse (to mom)..76

River 78
Anxious Alchemy 80
Godlessness 82
Ouroboros 84
Dielated..86
Boundless 88
Currentcy 90
As I Am...92
Sacra 94
To Witness 96
T-Shirt...98
On The Run 100
The Shackled 102
Yhwh Sings 104
A Voice 106
Barren Body...108
Nopales 110
Buzzin'...112
Quarrel 114
Figs 116
Om 118
Mold On The Fruits 120

iv. freedom costs   **123**
Freedom Costs 124
Half-Caff..126
Capital w/some ism 128
Cracked..130
G.M.Owed 132
Maggot..134
It Always Comes Back 134
Mercury 136
Iterations 138
Freedom With A Cost 140
That Hug...142
Thesis..144
Ripples..146
Fade Away 148
How 150
Plastic Bags 152
You will never know...154
A Day At The Beach...156
Cafes 158
Questions 4 a City 160

Death Instinct..162
Shred of Dread the Dead in my Head.......................................162

v. crying over spilt beer   165

Crying Over Spilt Beer...166
White Washed..168
Split..170
Self-Deconstructed 172
Daises On My Altar...174
Bridge Ashes...176
Xonochromatic 178
Akathreads 180
Conduit 182
Craving 184
Sanctuary 186
Time..188
Soulitude..190
Zapatos 192
Room 194
Mattress 196
The Soil of A Grave..198
Fractals 200
I Hope Your Garden Grows 202
Afterglow...204
Suffering 206
How Much Does Grief Cost? 208
Leave A Message At The..210
Fade 212
No Safety Net 212
Change 214
Vcr 216
Glow Glance..218
Sun Drunk..218
Hope 4 My Heart..220
Where You Water..222
Summer's Over..224
Non-Linear 226
Notes To Self 228
I Want To Die...230

i. personal history

we were sitting on the back porch when
the sound of his last empty beer got compressed into the concrete.
he leaned over with his breath smelling like brew and said
son, you have to break the chains because i couldn't. . .

WINGS OR CAGES

i know how to clean a wall until it turns
pearly white from smokey yellow.
i know how to read a face before
a bye or hello.

i know how to get hit with
words and fists and not react just so they stop.
i know how to stop being their entertainment.

i know that my dad's coffin has to be crammed
with everything he took to the grave and it probably
smells like cheap liquor & regret.

i know that love can be mistaken as lonliness and
attachment can be confused with being in love w/some1
who treats you just like those who abused you did.

i know that our maiden tongue was severed and a new1
was stitched back with tastebuds 4 exploited labor, land as
private property, and a blue-eyed-white-Jesus with long
wavy hair who looks like that Oakland hipster that rides his
bike and only drinks nitro cold brew at the cafe where i take
his order. i know that these imagined lines became borders.
i know that the people with the most things become hoarders.

i know that i don't know much but from what i do know
the stories that we tell ourselves can become our wings
                                        OR our cages.

WINGS OR CAGES

i know how to clean a wall until it turns
pearly white from smokey yellow.
i know how to read a face before
a bye or hello.

i know how to get hit with
words and fists and not react just so they stop.
i got tired from being their entertainment.

i know that my dad's coffin has to be crammed
with everything he took to the grave and it probably
smells like cheap liquor & regret.

i know that love can be mistaken as lonliness and
attachment can be confused with being in love w/some 1
who treats you just like those who abused you.

i know that our maiden tongue was severed and a new 1
was stitched back with tastebuds 4 exploited labor, land as
private property, and a blue-eyed-white-Jesus with long
wavy hair who looks like that Oakland hipster that rides his
bike and only drinks nitro cold brew at the cafe where i take
his order. i know that these imagined lines became borders.
i know that the people with the most things become hoarders.

i know that i don't know much but from what i do know
the ~~things~~ stories that we tell ourselves can become our wings
                                        OR our cages

PORTAL

the 1st home i had was in my mother's body of water
it was one of seven sacred seas of sons and daughters
it was oceanic how the tides pushed and pulled
for four planets who rose and ruled
with waves sounding like grieving
a heartbeat that silenced while leaving
the cluttered clouds were in the shape of lungs
the birds sung the sandy texture of a de ja vu rung
the salty taste that pinched like a dream
the wind it whispered and sowed a seam

i wonder if she knew —
she had an ocean swelling in her belly?
and that one day that ocean would return to itself
on the shore off the coast of California
contemplating its reflection

i wonder if she knew —
that each heartbeat was a stanza?
i wonder if she knew —
the more she sang the more i grew.
i wonder if she knew (with that mother's intuition)
that i was meant for more than our circumstance?
i wonder if she knew —
i was a seed in a grave
a lonely…lonely…wish in a wave

PORTAL ◎

the 1st home i had was in my mother's body of water
it was one of seven sacred seas of sons and daughters
it was oceanic how the tides pushed and pulled
for four planets who rose and ruled
with waves sounding like grieving
a ♡beat that silenced while leaving
the cluttered clouds were in the shape of lungs
the birds sung the sandy texture of a de ja vu rung
the salty taste that pinched like a dream
the wind it whispered and sowed a seam

i wonder if she knew —
she had an ocean swelling in her belly?
and that one day that ocean would return to itself
on the shore off the coast of California
contemplating its reflection

i wonder if she knew —
that each ♡beat was a stanza?
i wonder if she knew —
the more she sang the more i grew.
i wonder if she knew (with that mother's intuition)
that i was meant for more than our circumstance?
i wonder if she knew —
i was a seed in a grave
a lonely... lonely... wish in a wave

5

ETHEREAL

there was red mud on me at my birth
the sea salt child given from this earth
you cannot tell me what it is i'm worth
4 my worth is mine to decide

you see
i have oceans in my palms
and salt mines upon my cheeks
hidden treasures in my canyons
and journeys upon my peaks

i have
the heat of the desert
and the coolness of the sea
look into the bluest of skies
and then you'll see me

but don't get me wrong
i have lightning in these veins
thunder in my voice
striking in the rains
i have wind instead of whispers
roots instead of feet
redwood bark instead of skin
and water that is sweet

this is me

ETHEREAL

there was red mud on me at my birth
the sea salt child given from this earth
you cannot tell me what it is i'm worth
'4 my worth is mine to decide

you see
i have oceans in my palms
and salt mines upon my cheeks
hidden treasures in my canyons
and journeys upon my peaks

i have
the heat of the desert
and the coolness of the sea
look into the bluest of skies
and then you'll see me

but don't get me wrong
i have lightning in these veins
thunder in my voice
striking in the rains
i have wind instead of whispers
roots instead of feet
redwood bark instead of skin
and water that is sweet

this is me

HOME

displacement (n) - the moving of something from its place.

i didn't feel displaced but i didn't feel *in* place
i've never had *a* place
to call home
because home
was no home at all
it was more like juvenile hall
but without the daily meals or roll call
what it had in common was the warden and the cage
but the cage was non-physical and grew with age
and the warden was physical and was physical with rage
physical with words that you can't write on page
so they get written on the body like a tattoo that u hide
to remind YOU of the child in you that died
the child in you that cried
himself to sleep hoping that they dried when he awoke
but no. it was an ocean of tears that choked and provoked
the kicks and snares that beat your body where cps can't see
it makes you find a place in yourself where gps can't be
it makes you forget what happened to you
because remembering is too painful
speaking is too tiring
and getting close to anyone is too dangerous
so *home*
becomes where no one can touch you
but also a place where no one is invited

HOME

displacement (n) - the moving of something from its place.

i didn't feel displaced but i didn't feel in place
i've never had a place
to call home
because home
was no home at all
it was more like juvenile hall
but without the daily meals or roll call
what it had in common was the warden and the cage
but the cage was non-physical and grew with age
and the warden was physical and was physical with rage
physical with words that you can't write on page
so they get written on the body like a tattoo that u hide
to remind YOU of the child in you that died
the child in you that cried
himself to sleep hoping they dried when he awoke
but no. it was an ocean of tears that choked and provoked
the kicks and snares that beat your body where cps can't see
it makes you find a place in yourself where gps can't be
it makes you forget what happened to you
because remembering is too painful
speaking is too tiring
and getting close to anyone is too dangerous
so home
becomes where no one can touch you
but also a place where no one is invited

Not Long After

there was no, *i love you*
while i was being conceived.
there was only an apartment screen door closing
and a teenage romance being grieved.

not long after
i was a sad sigh after the 3rd pregnancy test.
not long after
i was a broken heartbeat in an ultrasound.

they say,
that i was a mistake.
i agree and say,
maternal chemicals told her to keep me.

i'm just another statistic
turned artistic
she was 17
it was the 90s
it was april 19th on the cusp
and my dad wasn't there because of a
he's not mine.

NOT LONG AFTER

there was no, "i love you"
while i was being conceived.
there was only an apartment door closing
and a teenage romance being grieved.

not long after
i was a sad sigh after the 3rd pregnancy test.
not long after
i was a broken heartbeat in an ultrasound.

they say,
that i was a mistake*
i agree and say
maternal chemicals ~~that~~ told her to keep me.

i'm just another statistic
turned artistic
she was 17
it was the 90s
it was APRIL 19th on the cusp
and my dad wasn't there because of a
~~he not mine.~~

SPIT & BONES

i try to swallow the
you're just like your dad
while trying to tame the tears.
mom. . . your words feel like they're being
forced down my throat like the peer pressured pills for
the despondent depression that doesn't have a label yet.

i try to SPIT out the
you're a loser and *you're worthless*
words because they've overstayed their welcome.
i'm trying to accept myself now
hating myself is yours and was my father's nature.

i learned it from you!
with your kind high pitched voice on the phone
and your low raspy tone when you're putting me down.

i learned it from him!
with his charming smile and telling people he loves them
to the size 12 shoe that was kicking me to stop crying.

SPIT & BONES

i try to swallow the
you're just like your dad
while trying to tame the tears.
mom... your words feel like they're being
forced down my throat like the peer pressured pills for
the despondent depression that doesn't have a label yet.

i try to SPIT out the
you're a loser and you're worthless
words because they've overstayed their welcome.
i'm trying to accept myself now
hating myself is yours and was my father's nature.

i learned it from you!
with your kind high pitched voice on the phone
and your low raspy tone when you're putting me down.

i learned it from him!
with his charming smile and telling people he loved him
to the size 12 shoe that was kicking me to stop crying.

2 BREAK UH PROMISE

most people don't know
i was homeless sleeping in a van
with my pops stealing on stolen land
by day he broke things and by night he broke down

the shell of a man but the tears of a boy
all of the fear but none of the joy
a tough exterior constructed by survival
the concrete walls always expected his arrival

you see, where my dad was from it was
superior or inferior
there were no in-betweens
just crack fiends and cracked screens
red and blue holes ripping through slacked jeans

it was broken windshields and vacant hotels that
smelled like chain smokers and ales
prison tattoos and kite tails
the cards were dealt and declined
the pain was felt and defined
but never processed
staying out the pen means
you progressed

broken homes to broken bones
2 break a dollar is 2 break uh promise

2 BREAK uh PROMISE

most people don't know
i was homeless sleeping in a van
with my pops stealing on stolen land
by day he broke things and by night he broke down

the shell of a man but the tears of a boy
all of the fear but none of the joy
a tough exterior constructed by survival
the concrete walls always expected his arrival

you see, where my dad was from it was
superior or inferior
there were no in-betweens
just ~~crack~~ crack fiends and cracked screens
red and blue holes ripping through slacked jeans

it was broken windshields and vacant hotels that
smelled like chain smokers and ales
prison tattoos and kite tails
the cards were dealt and declined
the pain was felt and defined
but never processed
staying out the pen means
you progressed

broken homes to broken bones
2 break a dollar is 2 break uh promise

BURNT CARPET

the smell of burnt carpet
and the sound of flesh being smacked
the taste of cup-of-noodles and
the sight of bags packed.

you have a gun with a bullet
who sounds out my name
the "soldier" tatted across the belly
has his aim.

with shaking hands
so quick to be this-triggered
it's no wonder why
your tongue gets disfigured.

vile and venemous
unstable and strenuous
i ran, you caught me
you ran, you taught me
being you, is not me
you got me then shot me
and shot me.

[i'll suffer my way to wisdom
if i can live long enough
the way this pain compresses me
i'm the diamond in the
dust]

16

BURNT CARPET

the smell of burnt carpet
and the sound of flesh being smacked
the taste of cup-of-noodles and
the sight of bags packed.

you have a gun with a bullet
who sounds out my name
the "S O L D I E R" tatted across the belly
has his ~~mis~~ aim.

with shaking hands
so quick to be this-triggered
its no wonder why
your tongue gets disfigured.

vile and venemous
unstable and strenuous
i ran, you caught me
you ran, you taught me
being you, is not me
you got me then shot me
and shot me.

i'll suffer my way to wisdom
if i can live long enough
the way this pain compasses me
i'm the diamond in the
dust

I'VE

i've made love 2 loneliness
in the midst of my despair
i've bit my nails and
i've buzzed my hair.

i've hurt people that loved me
and loved people that hurt me
i've pulled in people that ignored me
and pushed away people that heard me.

i've been ugly and selfish
and cruel and shattered hearts
i've held the healers and
cut my hands on their broken parts.

I'VE

i've made love 2 lonliness
in the midst of my despair
i've bit my nails and
i've buzzed my hair.

i've hurt people that loved me
and loved people that hurt me
i've pulled people in that ignored me
and pushed away people that heard me.

i've been ugly and selfish
and cruel and shattered hearts
i've held the healers and
cut my hands on their broken parts.

19

No Role Models

a grown man groomed me
when i was vulnerable and alone
and now when others try to touch me
i get evasive and unknown.

i was a teenager
yearning 4 role models
because all i had
was a father who could hold bottles
better than jobs.

it <u>was</u> confusing to see my dad
need something that abused him and not need me.
it <u>was</u> confusing to see my dad
use something that used him and not feed me.

but it makes sense now though
now that i'm his age.
i feel the rage.
i feel the shadows banging upon the cage
whispering and conspiring to steal the stage.
i try my best to not engage
not engage
not engage
turn the page
turn the page
turn the page

20

No Role Models

a grown man groomed me
when i was vulnerable and alone
and now when others try to touch me
i get evasive and unknown.

i was a teenager
yearning 4 role models
because all i had
was a father who could hold bottles
better than jobs.

it was confusing to see my dad
need something that abused and him and not need me
it was confusing to see my dad
use something that used him and not feed me.

but it makes sense now though
now that i'm his age.
i feel the rage.
i feel the shadows banging upon the cage
whispering and conspiring to steal the stage.
i try my best to not engage.
not engage
not engage
turn the page
turn the page
turn the page

I Remember

i remember strange men in and out my home
days when i was young and somehow free to roam.

i remember down the hall i'd hear my mother cry
sounds got lost somewhere and never found a why.

i remember my pops in and out a cell
i had to hide everything for my show and tell.

i remember being abandoned and used for some welfare
i gotta tell you it was hell there. . .
but we'd cope
we'd cope with some gloves and a bag
a ball and some hoops
P T S D
like some retired army troops

yeah i could have had it worse
i mean i could have had it great
but this is what it is
for those who can relate.

I REMEMBER

i remember strange men in and out my home
days when i was young and somehow free to roam.

i remember down the hall i'd hear my mother cry
sounds got lost somewhere and never found a why.

i remember my pops in and out a cell
i had to hide everything for my show and tell.

i remember being abundoned and wed for some welfare
i gotta tell you it was hell there...
but we'd cope
we'd cope with some gloves and a bag
a ball and some hoops
P T S D
like some retired army troops.

yeah i could have had it worse
i mean i could have had it great
but this is what it is
for those who can relate.

23

YOUR CONVENIENCE

you stole my youth and drank it down
until there wasn't nothing left for me
except to drown
in lamenting lows
and manic highs
those mechanic eyes
compulsive lies
stole something priceless
when i was vice-less voiceless
in a crisis

you exchanged my light for darkness
my fire that burned became spark-less
the last dying ember i can't remember
my essence was lost
held and bit by frost
feeling nothing at no cost
but my own

so
in the end
you found pleasure and i got pains
you got freedom and i got chains

at your convenience

YOUR CONVENIENCE

you stole my youth and drank it down
until there was nothing left for me
except to drown
in ~~senstive~~ lows
and manic highs
those mechanic eyes
~~compulsive~~ lies
stole something priceless
when i was vice-less voiceless
in a crisis

you exchanged my light for darkness
my fire that burned became spark-less
the last dying ember i can remember
my essence was lost
held and bit by frost
feeling nothing at no cost
but my own

so
in the end
you found pleasure and i got pains
you got freedom and i got chains

at your convenience

25

RORRIM

i fell through the cracks of concrete
but after some time i rose.
it was the free school lunches, the food stamps,
and the passed down clothes
that didn't fit.

it was the shame that turned into resentment that
found the self-hatred that i see today.
it was the empty fridges, the stolen money, and
the triggered memories that i cannot say.

it was the lack of father and the lack of guidance
that led me to this stranger in my mirror.
it was a long time that i hated who looked back
but now it's so much clearer. . .

RORRIM

i fell through the cracks of concrete
but after some time i rose.
it was the free school lunches, the food stamps,
and the passed down clothes
that didn't fit.

it was the shame that turned into resentment that
found the self-hatred that i see today.
it was the empty fridges, the stolen money, and
the triggered memories that i cannot say.

it was the lack of father and the lack of guidance
that led me to this stranger in the mirror.
it was a long time that i hated who looked back
but now it's so much clearer...

It Could Have Been

maybe it was the blunts at 11
that smoked out the shame?
or maybe it was the cheap stolen brandy
that never numbed the pain?

it could have been the abandonment
of my loved ones and people i needed?
it could have been the avoidance of lessons
that i never heeded?

it could have been the emptiness
that i tried to fill
with women, alcohol,
things, and out-of-date pills?

it could have been many things but
the exact cause of this depression
i may never know.

It Could Have Been

MAYBE IT WAS THE BLUNTS AT 11
THAT SMOKED OUT THE SHAME?
OR MAYBE IT WAS THE CHEAP STOLEN BRANDY
THAT NEVER NUMBED THE PAIN?

IT COULD HAVE BEEN THE ABANDONMENT
OF MY LOVED ONES AND PEOPLE I NEEDED?
IT COULD HAVE BEEN THE AVOIDANCE OF LESSONS
THAT I NEVER HEEDED?

IT COULD HAVE BEEN THE EMPTINESS
THAT I TRIED TO FILL
WITH WOMEN, ALCOHOL,
THINGS, AND OUT-OF-DATE PILLS?

IT COULD HAVE BEEN MANY THINGS BUT
THE EXACT CAUSE OF THIS DEPRESSION
I MAY NEVER KNOW.

THE KITCHEN LIGHTS

the roaches roamed the couches like
columbus roamed the seas
and they found a body of interest
in this america that was me.

you turn on the lights and they scatter like
crumbs of stale cocoa pebbles.

and like columbus they multiply to
divide and conquer rebels.

and like columbus they bring their
filth and plagues.

if you look closely you'll see
ships 4 legs!

THE KITCHEN LIGHTS

the roaches roamed the couches like
columbus roamed the seas
and they found a body of interest
in this america that was me.

you turn on the lights and they scatter like
crumbs of stale cocoa pebbles.

and like columbus they multiply to
divide and conquer rebels.

and like columbus they bring their
filth and plagues.

if you look closely you'll see
ships 4 legs!

GAVEL

i watch my world unravel
under the judge's gavel
and although the pepper spray
took my eyes away
it gave me clarity too

my life was not mine anymore
i was a number in a system
a name to be forgotten
apple rotten
to the barcode
to be bartered murdered martyred
chewed and chartered
4 false prophets
with true profits

my pops was here before
i see his footsteps before me in infrared
the road less traveled dead
beat bearing witness with bare feet
away from the white t's and affiliation
maybe 2 a time and space 4 reconciliation

i wonder
will my son end up here too?
i look in the blurry scratched mirror for answers
but i only see you.

GAVEL

i watch my world unravel
under the judges gavel
and although the pepper spray
took my eyes away
it gave me clarity too

my life was not mine anymore
i was a # in a system
a name to be forgotten
apple rotten
to the barcode
to be bartered murdered martyred
chewed and chartered
4 false prophets
with true profits

my pops was here before
i see his footsteps before me in infrared
the road less traveled dead
beat bearing witness with bare feet
away from the white t's and affiliation
maybe 2 a time and space 4 reconciliation

i wonder
my will my son end up here too?
i look in the blurry crack scratched mirror for answers
but i only see you.

33

Mirage

running out of gas
we had to walk through the desert
the scars on my feet still ache
ghost pains i still remember

to this day
i still can't sleep in cars

i'm not 28 anymore i'm 11
sitting in the shade on a curb
watching my hero ask for money
a sight i can't forget, i sit hungry

the man who gave us a 20 had a sadness in his eyes
when he looked at me.

a mirage of a memory.

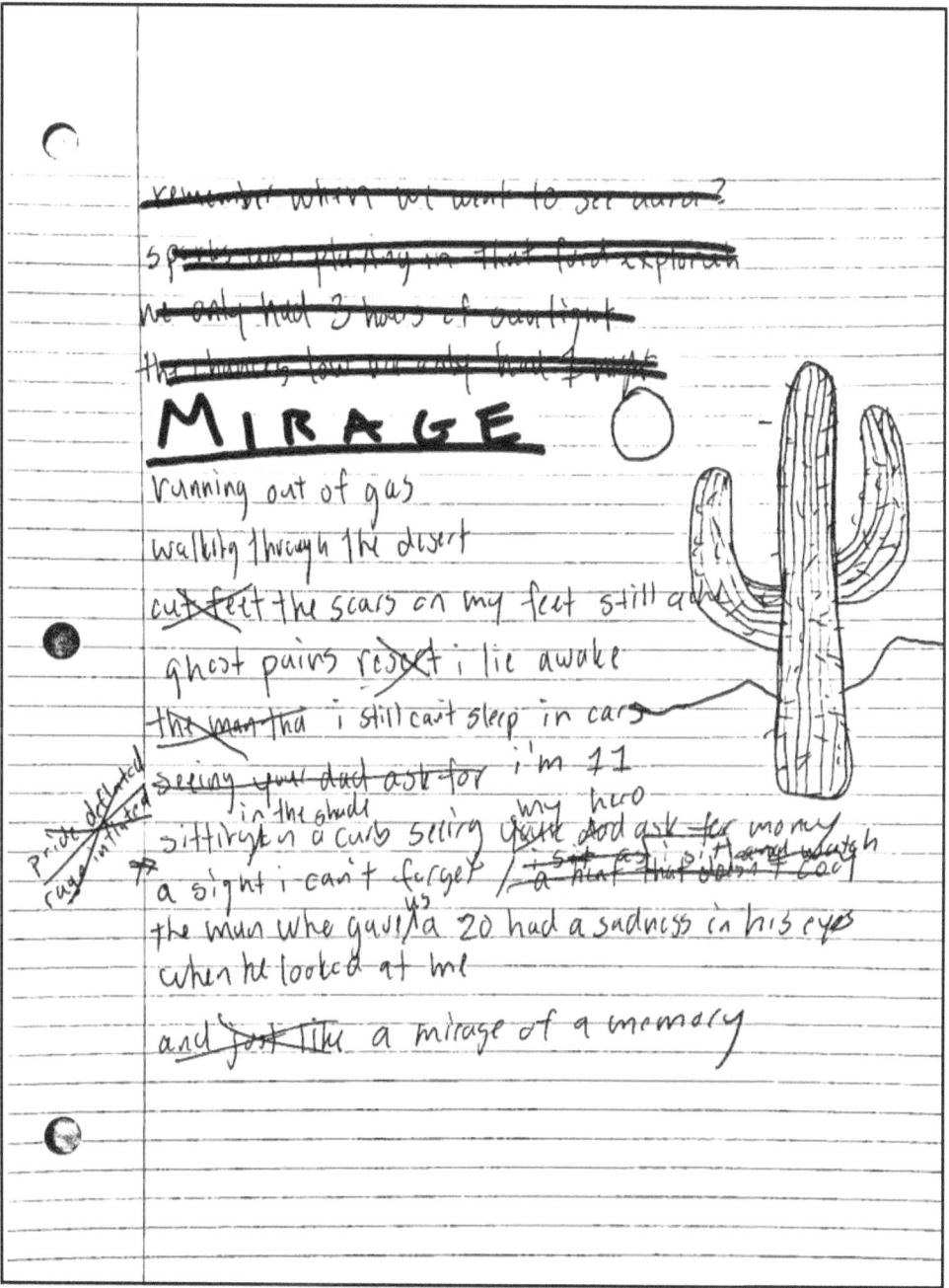

~~remember when we went to see dara?~~

~~speeding pit stop in that ford explorer~~

~~we only had 3 hours of sunlight~~

~~the ~~

MIRAGE

running out of gas
walking through the desert
cut ~~feet~~ the scars on my feet still ache
ghost pains resurt i lie awake
~~the man tha~~ i still can't sleep in cars

~~seeing your dad ask for~~ i'm 11
in the shade   my hero
sitting on a curb seeing ~~your dad ask for~~ money
a sight i can't forget / ~~a ~~

the man who gave us a 20 had a sadness in his eyes
when he looked at me

and ~~just like~~ a mirage of a memory

~~pride defeated~~
~~rage inflated~~

DEADICATION

work boot
floret on the fragile bottles like gas pedals
watch the glistening of glass petals
sprinkle against the sun-dried asphalt
the sound of aluminum being crushed & hospital rushed
into garbage bags i'm zipping bags and ripping rags
to riches CDs saying "GET RICH OR DIE TRYING"
but we stay poor in this plastic four door
that bumps and shakes like cali quakes
the eerie grind of squealing brakes
so salvaged
is my name like the title of our car
chipped shoulder paint and key scratched scars
faded tinted swells 3D printed cells
a dried puddle of bloody carpet stains
the leaking veins
the sunroof wanes
the rearview chains
the past appears closer than it is
i'm meant to be anywhere that isn't here. . . on the
grasses morning dew // mourning by picking poison
that reminds me of you. i'm drinking in //
your lost grave while listening to lost tapes instead
of resting in peace
you're in pieces scattered amongst beaches
scattered amongst leaches and tire screeches
holding molding grapes grasping onto gravel
casting stones with puking bones that turn 2 gavels

drunk. O-D. crash. SLOW-LY. dead. whiplash.

DEADICATION

work boot
floret on the fragile bottles like gas pedals
watch the glistening of glass petals
sprinkle against the sun-dried asphalt
the sound of aluminum being crushed & hospital rushed
into garbage bags i'm zipping bags and ripping rags
to riches CDs saying "GET RICH OR DIE TRYING"
but we stay poor in this plastic four door
that bumps and shakes like cali quakes
the eerie grind of squeaking brakes
so salvaged
is my name like the title of of our car
chipped shoulder paint and key scratched scars
~~fuck~~ faded tinted swells 3D printed cells
a dried puddle of bloody carpet stains
the leaking veins
the sunroof wanes
the rearview chains
the past appears closer than it is
i'm meant to be anywhere that isn't here... on the
grasses morning due // mourning by picking poison
that reminds me of you. i'm drinking in //
your lost grave while listening to lost 2upcs instead
of resting in peace
you're in pieces scattered amongst beaches
scattered amongst leaches and tire screeches
holding molding grapes grasping onto gravel
casting stones with puking bones that turn 2 gavels

drunk. O-D. crash. SLOW-LY. dead. whiplash.

37

ii. here nor there

memories come back in flashes.
fragments of scenes. in most of them
i don't know how i old i am
or if the memory actually happened.

FRAGMENTED

rusty rants run rampant round the room
dancing demons demanding doom.
they're growing gross of getting groomed
their bellowing bellies are being bloomed.

your mind may have forgotten
but your body recollects the
specs on spectacles that
sketched into skeptical.

those memories of colonizing hands
on petrified pores
2 triggered 2 distorted 2 be configured. . .
i'm flinching to the touch
fear doesn't need much.

there's variety in violence in the knuckles of hurricanes
the open palm of earthquakes and the tears of tsunamis
where recollection become fable
folded origami and unstable
i'm unable to
ask and ever tell tales of the scale
of scars that read like braille.

this is to my fragmented youth
that has fragmented me
and has fragmented you.

FRAGMENTED

rusty rants run rampant round the room
dancing demons demanding doom.
they're growing gross of getting groomed.
their bellowing bellies are being bloomed.

your mind may have forgotten
but your body recollects the
specs on spectacles that
sketched into skeptical.

those memories of colonizing hands
on petrified pores
2 triggered 2 distorted 2 be configured.
i'm flinching to the touch
fear doesn't need much.

there's variety in violence in the knuckles of hurricanes
the open palm of earthquakes and the tears of tsunamis
where recollection becomes table
folded origami and unstable
i'm unable to
ask and ever tell tales of the scale
of scars that read like braille.

this is to my fragmented youth
that has fragmented me
and has fragmented you.

DISSOLVE

with collapsing shoulders
and dissolving tongues
i feel you fill your resolving lungs

the sealing of lips
the sinking of ships
sailing
to somewhere beyond
the scars that hold stories
you don't embrace

the gloomy guest
with ear to chest
hand to breast with slight compress
it's hard to rest when
the rest of you is restless

i'm too busy to be tired
too tired to be busy
too broke to be ill
too anxious to be still
either way or any way
what does of any of it matter?
when darkness bends and light shatters
my particles to the point of scatters

the universe is dead and we're its dream

DISSOLVE

with collapsing shoulders
and dissolving tongues
i feel you fill your resolving lungs

the sealing of lips
the sinking of ships
sailing
to somewhere beyond
the scars that hold stories
you don't embrace

the gloomy guest
with ear to chest
hand to breast with slight compress
its hard to rest when
the rest of you is restless

i'm too busy to be tired
too tired to be busy
too broke to be ill
too anxious to be still
either way or any way
what does any of it matter?
when darkness bends and light shatters
my particles to the point of scatters

the universe is dead and we're its dream

COMPOST

i would crawl from this grave
if it's love that you gave
but instead i lay as compost
rotting in waves
watching
my skin swell
pale as seashells
on the seashore of my bloated organs

the tide pushes and pulls me
to a wakeless sleep that lulls me

no more fighting no more trying
just lying amongst the damp sand
in the stillness of dying

no more pain no more misery
i'm going back to oneness and fluidity

the seagulls and flies
will see the last of these cries
i'll return to the ocean
out the corner of these eyes

goodbye to all who i love
i hope
i'm more useful to you this way

COMPOST

i would crawl from this grave
if it's love that you gave
but instead i lay as compost
rotting in waves
watching my skin swell
pale as seashells
on the seashore of my bloated organs

the tide pushes and pulls me
to a wakeless sleep that lulls me

no more fighting no more trying
just lying amongst the damp sand
in the stillness of dying

no more pain no more misery
i'm going back to 1ness and fluidity

the seagulls and flies
will see the last of these cries
i'll return to the ocean
out the corner of these eyes

goodbye to all who i love
& hope
i'm more useful to you this way

YOUR SURFACE WORLD

because your impulses are your master
and your cavities come from gossip
i will not kiss your lips

because your oceans are shallow
and your tears are polluted
i will not swim in your waters

and because you only see your idea of me and not me
i will not show you this heart

for i am so much more

YOUR SURFACE WORLD

because your impulses are your master
and your cavities come from gossip
i will not kiss your lips

because your oceans are shallow
and your tears are polluted
i will not swim in your waters

and because you only see your idea of me and not me
i will not show you this heart

for i am so much more

47

I Am Frail

my skin scurries to the corners of the room.
my eyes watch the flowers die and bloom.
my hands weep from self-betrayal.
i am frail.

my tears evaporate before they hit the floor.
my legs always know their way to the door.
my fingers weep from self-betrayal.
i am frail.
i am frail.

my tongue speaks in knots.
i hear the plans and plots
get louder like pans and pots
trying to scrub away the sunset bruised spots.
my fingernails weep from self-betrayal.
i am frail
i am frail
i am frail

i am frail

my skin scurries to the corner of the room.
my eyes watch the flowers die and bloom.
my hands weep from self-betrayal.
i am frail.

my tears evaporate before they hit the floor.
my legs always know their way to the door.
my fingers weep from self-betrayal.
i am frail.
i am frail.

my tongue speaks in knots
i hear the plans and plots
get louder like pans and pots
trying to scrub away the sunset bruised spots.
~~my~~ my fingernails weep from self-betrayal.
i am frail.
i am frail.
i am frail.

49

Colors

my bones are
skittles shaken like dice
my sister got lice
again, we're beaten
starburst pink

can't candy coat judicial ink

tio's smokin' purple, i think
momma's feelin' blue
so she bleaches away the brown
i put my mongoose down
and it got stolen

cops rollin'

step-dad is green as grass
freshly mowed skippin' class
i barely pass
yellow tape
white tees
black beanies
nikes

yellow teeth in a black robe
red eyes reading j*obe*
pale faces fill spaces
where orange threads hold drooped heads
beige court cases fold grouped beds

50

COLORS

my bones are
skittles shaken like dice
my sister got lice
again, we're beaten
starburst pink

can't candy coat judicial ink
tio's smokin' purple, i think
momma's feelin' blue
so she bleaches away the brown
i put my mongoose down
and it got stolen

cops rollin'

step-dad is green as grass
freshly mowed skippin' class
i barely pass
yellow tape
white tees
black beanies
nikes

yellow teeth in a black robe
red eyes reading jobe
pale faces fill spaces
where oarnge threads hold drooped heads
beige court cases fold grouped beds

51

HOLD

you've been held so long
you forgot how to hold
when i ask for your warmth
all i get is the cold

you say you don't have space for me
i have oceans, deserts, rivers, and valleys
bridges, skylines, main streets, and alleys
for you

somewhere inside of me wishes i could have the same
kind of room
to be faulty
to be needy
to be hurt
to be greedy
to be myself

i'm tired of shapeshifting for your moods.
i know it's my fault.
i know it's on me.
i know i'm to blame.
i know. i know. i can see
that i love you so much
that i'd put myself aside
even when i need you
to hold me.

HOLD

you've been held so long
you forgot how to hold
when i ask for your warmth
all i get is the cold

you say you don't have space for me
i have oceans, deserts, rivers, and valleys
bridges, sky lines, main streets, and alleys
for you

somewhere inside of me wishes i could have the same
kind of room
to be faulty
to be needy
to be hurt
to be greedy
to be myself

i'm tired of shapeshifting for your moods.
i know it's my fault.
i know it's on me.
i know i'm to blame.
i know. i know. i can see
that i love you so much
that i'd put myself aside
even when i need you
to hold me.

DOMESTIC SILENCE

i didn't know rage
until my mom was punched in her ribcage
it was the first time i wanted someone dead
the first time i seen red
it was a timestamp
in slow motion
i was 15
maybe 16
my sister tackled me
hole in the wall couldn't spackle me
screaming murder
i would have stabbed him
fists exchanging his grandma grabbed him
dirt or soil
water oil
character foil
no resurrection
or court objection
the kid always in a u-haul
watching his single mother in a pool hall
no dad to call
a boy told two words
do all

DOMESTIC SILENCE

i didn't know rage
until my mom was punched in her ribcage
it was the first time i wanted someone dead
the first time i seen red
it was a timestamp
in slow motion
i was 15
maybe 16
my sister tackled me
hole in the wall couldn't spackle me
screaming murder
i would have stabbed him
fists exchanging his grandma grabbed him
dirt or soil
water oil
character foil
no resurrection
or court objection
the kid always in a u-haul
watching his single mother in a pool hall
no dad to call
a boy told two words
do all

PARALLEL

i feel like we
loved each other many times in a parallel
full circle every time we carousel

i hide in oceans
and you hold me in my dreams
our auras embrace like the wind does the trees

i'm only a call away
a courageous touch that goes beyond what we know
a few words that says what we show

i wonder if you feel this way too?
this incomplete feeling
this void that can't be filled
this hope that maybe
we're each other's "one"

PARALLEL

i feel like we
loved each other many times in a parallel
full circle every time we carousel

i hide in oceans
and you hold me in my dreams.
our auras embrace like the wind does the trees

i'm only a call away
a courageous touch that goes beyond what we know
a few words that says what we show

i & wonder if you feel this way too?
this incomplete feeling
this void that can't be filled
this hope that maybe
we're each other's "one"

NOTHING FEELS REAL

lately i don't feel real
i don't feel here

i feel like i'm back in the cul-de-sac
bruises on my nose and back
aching
they said they're making
me tough
making me tough
tears like the tide
taking a puff
bammer in shoe paper
turns to vapors for da f
street ball no ref
double rim
no net
astral
project away from the pain
headphones blaring numbing the brain
nightmares nightly
i wake up gasping for air
daymares daily
i take up grasping for care
that i'll never receive
i hear nice words
that i'll never believe

NOTHING FEELS REAL

lately i don't feel real
i don't feel here

i feel like i'm back in the culdesac
bruises on my nose and back
aching
they said they're making
me tough
making me tough
tears like the tide
taking a puff
bammer in shoe paper
turns to vapors for da f
street ball no ref
double rim
no net
astral
project away from the pain
headphones blaring numbing the brain
nightmares nightly
i wake up gasping for air
daymares daily
i take up grasping for care
that i'll never receive
i hear nice words
that i'll never believe

WORLDS' AWAY

the gray iron rattles
on the rusty threads
repetitions by beds
burpees from burnt brown carpet that hasn't been vacuumed
to a ceiling the color and texture of eggshells
pale skin under the leg cells
the chopping fan flutters
the black screen doors are pounded followed by chihuahua mutt mutters
the *Me Against The World* cd skips
DVD rips boyish hands turning them to grips
scuffed forces too big for my feet on pegs of stolen bikes
fishing rods down hills on these concrete hikes
macy bags without receipts
it all repeats it all repeats it all repeats
but doesn't skip like Pac
all these memories that can't talk
i'm:
worlds' away from collecting liquor bottles
worlds' away from blacking out at twelve years old
worlds' away from EBT cards and asking for money
world's away from sleeping with roaches and molesting coaches
world's away from bandos and tweakers
worlds' away from predatory preachers
worlds' away from muggin' in photos
i'm worlds' away
but the memories weigh
more than i can carry

WORLDS' AWAY

the gray iron rattles
on the rusty threads
repetitions by beds
burpees from burnt brown carpet that hasn't been vacuumed
to a ceiling the color and texture of eggshells
pale skin under the leg cells
the chopping fan flutters
the black screen doors are pounded followed by chihuahua mutt mutter
the *Me Against the World* cd skips
DVD rips boyish hands turning them to grips
scuffed forces too big for my feet on pegs of stolen bikes
fishing rods down hills on these concrete hikes
macy bags without receipts
it all repeats it all repeats it all repeats
but doesn't skip like Pac
all these memories that can't talk
i'm:
worlds' away from collecting liquor bottles
worlds' away from blacking out at twelve years old
worlds' away from EBT cards and asking for money
worlds' away from sleeping with roaches and molesting coaches
worlds' away from bundles and tweakers
worlds' away from predatory preachers
worlds' away from muggin' in photos
i'm worlds' away
but the memories weigh
more than i can carry

i Think i Was 8

i contemplate
the last time i felt young
i think i was 8
riding my bike
it was late
the street lights were about to flicker on
rushing home before momma bickers on
if she's even there
no one cares
she's usually out at night or sleeping through the day
or "around the corner" when we call
me and my sisters are cleaning walls
now we're cleaning grout
what is this about?
we always shout
instead of talking
they stole my bike so back to walking
i'm always at my best friend's house cause it's peaceful
he's an only child with all the games
has a year book signed with all the names
his mom brings him snacks
his dad takes him to the store
i tag along seeing more
of what a family can be
ring ring ring
my mom calls
it's time to go back home

i THINK i WAS 8

i contemplate
the last time i felt young
i ~~w~~ think i was 8
riding my bike
it was late
the street lights were about to flicker on
rushing home before momma bickers on
if she's even there
no one cares
she's usually out at night or sleeping through the day
or "around the corner" when we call
me and my sisters are cleaning walls
now we're cleaning grout
what is this about?
we always shout
instead of talking
they stole my bike so back to walking
i'm always at my best friend's house cause its peaceful
he's an only child with all the games
has a year book signed with all the names
his mom brings him ~~snacks~~ snacks
his dad takes him to the store
i tag along seeing more
of what a family can be
ring ring ring!
my mom calls
it's time to go back home

63

I WAS 4TEEN

it was summer
freshmen year came to a close
i went back to see an old caretaker
back in Fresno
he didn't have a place for me to sleep
so i stayed at his friend's
she was 23
i was 14
and a virgin
conditioning and chemicals started merging
she started urging
me to smoke
then made a pass at me as a joke
then she left to work
and came back in the shadows of the doorway
i was still high and now she was tipsy
i should want this right? (she starts grinding up against me)
sex is all a 14-year-old thinks about right? (she takes off my shorts)
this is something to brag about to my boys right? (i get on top of her)
can't remember more
she goes to sleep and i lay there
feeling empty and thinking to myself, "was that *it*?"

for years i told myself that i wasn't taken advantaged of
but i think back now and feel the wound of being used

64

i was 4teen

it was summer
freshmen year came to a close
i went back to see an old caretaker
back in FRESNO
he didn't have a place for me to sleep
so i stayed at his friend's
she was 25
i was 14
and a virgin
conditioning and chemicals started merging
she started urging
me to smoke
then made a pass at me as a joke
then she left to work
and came back in the shadows of the doorway
i was still high and now she was tipsy
i should want this right? (she starts grinding up against me)
sex is all a 14 year old thinks about right? (she takes off my shorts)
this is something to brag about to my boys right? (i get on top of her)
i can't remember anymore
she goes to sleep and i lay there
feeling empty and thinking to myself, "was that it?"

for years i told myself that i wasn't taken advantage of
but i think back now and feel the wound of being used

ANCESTORS

i don't have ancestors
ain't nobody guiding me
my roots been cut compass gut
i'm a mutt i'm despising me
mixed
with indigenous disposition
colonizing missions with white stucco walls
red clay tiles for a roof
aloof
my daddy died from 80proof
poof
ain't nobody sober
ain't nobody care
life ain't fair or fluid it's stupid
it's fixed and rigid as concrete on feet on streets
cracking jokes like knuckles the city chuckles
baggy pants hide when knees buckle under generational gravity
depravity, i'm bound 2 die here
so i lie here in my fear
that
can't be voiced by a colonized tongue
can't be written by shackled hands
can't be witnessed by a guilty lens
can't simply be
in a society that doesn't have my wellbeing in mind
so no, i don't have ancestors
ain't nobody guiding me

ANCESTORS

i don't have ancestors
ain't nobody guiding me
my roots been cut compass gut
i'm a mutt i'm despising me
mixed
with indigenous disposition
colonizing missions with white stucco walls
red clay tiles for a roof
aloof
my daddy died from 80proof
poof
ain't nobody sober
ain't nobody care
life ain't fair or fluid it's stupid
it's fixed and rigid as concrete on feet on streets
cracking jokes like knuckles the city chuckles
baggy pants hide when knees buckle under generational gravity
depravity, i'm bound 2 die here
so i lie here in my fear
that
can't be voiced by a colonized tongue
can't be written by shackled hands
can't be witnessed by a guilty lens
can't simply be
in this society that doesn't have my wellbeing in mind
so no, i don't have ancestors
ain't nobody guiding me

WORDS THEY SAY

my older sister tells me "take care of my daughter" after swallowing a
bottle of pills and then hanging up.
my dad tells me "i love you" before he ODs and the next time i
see him tubes are the only thing keeping him alive.
my mom tells me that i need to accept jesus into my heart and
until i do i'll keep having the nightmares that make me gasp for air.
my uncle tells me "stop being a little bitch."
my tia tells me "don't be a snitch."
my grandma tells me "you look just like your dad."
my cousin tells me "you're such a fucking crybaby"
years later that same cousin tells me the four other cousins we grew up
with got locked up, shot, addicted to something, and/or ended up on the
most wanted list.
my ex tells me "you're taking up too much space."
my friend tells me "have you every considered some therapy?"
my boy tells me "it's all mental."
my coworker tells me "sometimes, you're like a dark cloud to be
around." my boss tells me "you can't come to work late" and "we need
you to be more productive." my body tells me "i'm tired."
my roommate tells me "you intimidate me."
my depression tells me "just kill yourself and this will all be over."
my inner child tells me "let's go on adventures and have fun."
my inner adult replies "we don't have the time or money."
my intuition tells me "trust me, just keep going."
my psyche tells me "you should really try therapy again."

and everyone else tells me "you sound like you're doing great!"

68

WORDS THEY SAY

my older sister tells me "take care of my daughter" after swallowing a bottle of pills and then hanging up.
my dad tells me "i love you" before he ODs and the next time i see him tubes are the only thing keeping him alive.
my mom tells me that i need to accept jesus into my heart and until i do i'll keep having the nightmares that make me gasp for air.
my uncle tells me "stop being a little bitch"
my tia tells me "don't be a snitch."
my grandma tells me "you look just like your dad."
my cousin tells me "you're such a fucking crybaby"
years later that same cousin tells me the four other cousins we grew up with got locked up, shot, addicted to something, and/or ended up on the most wanted list.
my ex tells me tells me "you're taking up too much space."
my friend tells me "have you ever considered some therapy?"
my boy tells me "it's all mental."
my coworker tells me "sometimes, you're like a dark cloud to be around." my boss tells me "you can't come to work late" and "we need you to be more productive." my body tells me "i'm tired."
my roommate tells me "you intimidate me."
my depression tells me "just kill yourself and this will all be over."
my inner child tells me "lets go on adventures and have fun."
my inner adult replies "we don't have the time or money."
my intuition tells me "trust me, just keep going."
my psyche tells me "you should really try therapy again."

and everyone else tells me "you sound like you're doing great!"

69

Neither Here Nor There

dna says indigenous
skin says spanish
when they ask me "what are you?"
i wish i could vanish
because i don't know what i am
"i'm mexican" i say
"where is your family from?" they say
"i don't know" i shrug
"habla espanol?"
"no, my parents didn't teach me. i'm americanized"

i'm not mexican enough to be mexican
i don't speak spanish and my family calls me güero
and even though my
great-grandfather was a bracero
it's only my pale face that they see
i'm not brown enough to be POC
a shade too light to take up any spaces
but not white enough for anglo faces
i'm "racially ambiguous"
living in a world in between

i'm neither here nor there
i'm neither here nor there
i'm neither here nor there
i don't belong anywhere

NEITHER HERE NOR THERE

dna says indigenous
skin says spanish
when they ask me "what are you?"
i wish i could vanish
because i don't know what i am
"i'm mexican" i say
"where is your family from?" they say
"i don't know" i shrug
"habla espanol?"
"no, my parents didn't teach me, i'm americanized"

i'm not mexican enough to be mexican
i don't speak spanish and my family calls me güero
and even though my
great-grandfather was a bracero
it's only my pale face that they see
i'm not brown enough to be POC
a shade too light to take up any spaces
but not white enough for anglo faces
i'm "racially ambiguous"
living in a world in between

i'm neither here nor there
i'm neither here nor there
i'm neither here nor there
i don't belong anywhere

71

iii. the infinite

so many tears from all my faces
they waterfall to seashores
upon these laces
double knotted to hold the spaces

CROWS (TO MY POPS)

when you died
you taught me how to live
when you lied
there
grief showed me how to give
from the summit of my happiness
to the depth of my despair
i see your movements in the crows
i hear your whispers in the air
i taste your laugh in the broken family dinners
i smell the sweat from the 1 on 1 basketball games
i miss you
and i love you because you were my first hero
and i resent you because you were my first villain

i truly hope the wind carried your ashes to a place
where you found some stillness and some grace
because i had to create that here
alone
after the last thing you asked me was
"can you send me some money?" on the phone
(i didn't know what to say so i said nothing)
and then after a long silence you said "i love you, son" *click*
the next thing i knew the doctors asked me to pull the plug quick
decision in a moment that needed years to process
but a choice had to be made and i have to live with it
while you had to die with it

CROWS (TO MY POPS)

when you died
you taught me how to live
when you lied
there
grief showed me how to give
from the summit of my happiness
to the depth of my despair
i see your movements in the crows
i hear your whispers in the air
i taste your laughs in the broken family dinners
i smell the sweat from the 1 on 1 basketball games
i miss you
and i love you because you were my first hero
and i resent you because you were my first villain

i truly hope the wind carried your ashes to a place
where you found some stillness and some grace
because i had to create that here
alone
after the last thing you asked me was
"can you send me some money?" on the phone
(i didn't know what to say so i said nothing)
and then after a long silence you said, "i love you, son" *click*
the next thing i knew the doctors asked me to pull the plug quick
decision in a moment that needed years to process
but a choice had to be made and i have to live with it
while you had to die with it

LUNAR ECLIPSE (TO MOM)

to see the freedom upon your face
was like seeing an angel in their grace
your wings had feathers of luminous light
that made me feel that all was right.

you have suffered your entire life
you deserve this prosperity
you deserve to know peace
and to know clarity
and release.

you have been a god trusting woman
who has carried the burden of pain
so for this moment i ask you
dance in this rain
even if it is your tears.

you have given your years
for us and for them
it's your turn to feel your love
i love you mom
amen.

p.s. everywhere i go i know you're not far away

LUNAR ECLIPSE (TO MOM)

to see the freedom upon your face
was like seeing an angel in their grace
your wings had feathers of luminous light
that made me feel that all was right.

you have suffered your entire life
you deserve this prosperity
you deserve to know peace
and to know clarity
and release.

you have been a god trusting woman
who has carried the burden of pain
so for this moment i ask you
dance in this rain
even if it is your tears!

you have given your years
for us and for them
its your turn to feel your love
i love mom
amen.

p.s. everywhere i go i know you're not far away

RIVER

like the river that speaks in a thousand voices
my life flows downstream to a thousand choices
this use to bring me grief but now it brings me peace
the bondage of fighting the current slow release
surrender

the water always returns
it is not bound to time like this body
so as it is
one day i will return to you
and you will do the same
and we will be in oneness
at birth with our graves
in the om of waves

my soul
knows the omens, the symbols, the signs
because intuition is a present current
by design
the stillness of streams
the remembering of dreams
everything is everything
it seems

this life is a thief
in my resolve i am a leaf
falling to the river

RIVER

like the river that speaks in a thousand voices
my life flows downstream to a thousand choices
this use to bring me grief but now it brings me peace
the bondage of fighting the current slow release
surrender

the water always returns
it is not bound to time like this body
so as it is
one day i will return to you
and you will do the same
and we will be in oneness
at birth with our graves
in the om of waves

my soul
knows the omens, the symbols, the signs
because intuition is a present current
by design
the stillness of streams
the remembering of dreams
everything is everything
it seems

this life is a thief
in my resolve i am a leaf
falling to the river

ANXIOUS ALCHEMY

smudged makeup like the smudged sage
i'm so glad that i met you at your judged stage
the final rapture recaptured in your chiseled cage
drizzled rage on the spineless backs of bridges that
always break easily without consent. to forgive or to resent?
there is no dent in the strength of these structures
there is only necessity for them to crumble
destroy. build. destroy. what comes after?

you see these bridges i've walked over are made of many
the lovers the silenced the oppressed
plenty of perfect prisons overtly obsessed
with overcrowding numbers abolished compressed
too polished is the ineffable proudly expressed
it's the american way they say of asserting power
hospitable grins that end backstabbingly sour
is the sweetness of privileged freedom
why would one ever want to perceive
reality for what it truly is?
to have this life means someone else can't
the impermanence of this body i feel in the protest chants
to survive to sonder
to assume form to ponder
to dissolve to wander
to trade headaches for heartaches
to trade you my numbness
for your heartbreaks

ANXIOUS ALCHEMY

smudged makeup like the smudged sage
i'm so glad that i met you at your judged stage
the final rapture recaptured in your chiseled cage
drizzled rage on the spineless backs of bridges that
always break easily without consent. to forgive or to resent?
there is no dent in the strength of these structures
there is only neccessity for them to crumble
destroy. build. destroy. what comes after?

you see these bridges i've walked over are made of many
the lovers the silenced the oppressed
plenty of perfect prisons overtly obsessed
with overcrowding numbers abolished compressed
too polished is the ineffable proudly expressed
its the american way they say of asserting power
hospitable grins that end backstabbingly sour
is the sweetness of privileged freedom
why would one ever want to perceive
reality for what it truly is?
to have this life means someone else can't
the impermanence of this body i feel in the protest chants
to survive to sonder
to assume form to ponder
to dissolve to wander
to trade headaches for heartaches
to trade you my numbness
for your heartbreaks

GODLESSNESS

sometimes it seems
like we're living in hell
the scars and unhealed wounds upon this shell.

the godlessness.
the lovelessness.
the grim denial of mortality.
maybe we're meant to suffer?

this is our wasteland. our consequence.
our daymare and night terrors come to life.
it's time reap what imperialism has sowed.
pay what you owe. receive what you're owed.

the sorrowful road.

from sunrise to sunset
stuck in my minuscule perception.
there is no gleaming moon
just an optical illusion from my mind's deception.

in the end, all that is left is hopelessness
or the delusion of hope.
a vacancy resides in this deteriorating body.
i can't cope. there is no use in trying to fight it.

GODLESSNESS

sometimes it seems
like we're living in hell
the scars and unhealed wounds upon this shell.

the godlessness.
the lovelessness.
the grim denial of mortality.
maybe we're meant to suffer?

this is our wasteland. our consequence.
our daymare and night terrors come to life.
its time to reap what imperialism has sowed.
pay what you owe. receive what you're owed.

the sorrowful road.

from sunrise to sunset
stuck in my minuscule perception.
there is no gleaming moon
just an optical illusion from my mind's deception.

in the end, all that is left is hopelessness
or the delusion of hope.
a vacancy resides in this deteriorating body.
i can't cope. there is no use in trying to fight it.

OUROBOROS

i'm deposited like a check
to this prison atm
like all before me i am
undesirable to even the
most nurturing of hands

you don't think that
we're connected but that's
a manufactured loop
like puffed circle hoops 4carrots ice cream scoops
hanging without merit at lake merritt
walking to bare it with bare feet on concrete
from names fading on streets

to organize is to move mountains
to mobilize is to break structures
repair ruptures hissing punctures
in ribcage cracks
slithering bullets getting smacked
concussion rattles helmet sacked
crystallized immortalized
i'm mortified

it seems
i'm not who i thought i was

OUROBOROS

i'm deposited like a check
to this prison atm
like all before me i am
undesirable to even the
most nurturing of hands

you don't think that
we're connected but that's
a manufactured loop
like puffed circle hoops 4carrots ice cream scoops
hanging without merit at Lake Merritt
walking to bare it with bare feet on concrete
from names fading on streets

to organize is to move mountains
to mobilize is to break structures
repair ruptures hissing punctures
in ribcage cracks
slithering bullets getting smacked
concussion rattles helmet sacked
crystallized immortalized
i'm mortified

it seems
i'm not who i thought i was

DIELATED

if i lived here in singularity
and dissolved on your tongue like acid
would you help me leave this placid place?

you love dancing
and you make me love dancing, too.
when you move we move in two
now all i see is blue.

you don't want to live
and i mirror that projection.
all we've known is survival and protection
not asymmetrical reflection.

how you make fists turn to open palms
and tongues sing psalms
and how you make skin calm
and soft as cotton candy
is beyond my understanding.

you garden-grown-beautifully-rooted being
blessed and aligned and all-seeing.
your strands of love flow like
the hair you always cut, buzz, dye
you never even need a who, what, or why
so when i—look you in the eye
my essence gets high.

DIELATED

if i lived here in singularity
and dissolved on your tongue like acid
would you help me leave this placid place?

you love dancing
and you make me love dancing too.
when you move we move in two
now all i see is blue.

you don't want to live
and i mirror that projection.
all we've known is survival and protection
not asymmetrical reflection.

how you make fists turn to open palms
and tongues sing psalms
and how you make skin calm
and soft as cotton candy
is beyond my understanding.

you garden-grown-beautifully-rooted being
blessed and aligned and all-seeing.
your strands of love flow like
the hair you always cut, buzz, dye
you never even need a who, what, or why
so when i — look in you in the eye
my essence gets high.

BOUNDLESS

boundless are your seas
and limitless are your depths
countless are the memories
birthing all the deaths

empty and calm is your mind
and still are your chants
watered evenly is your soil
quenched are your plants

a guardian of the light
and a creature of the dark
there is a mind out there
in need of a spark

so when you enter this unknown
know you are no stranger to the waves
in the midst of a memory
a heart that craves

to be more than what it is and less of what it's not
you long to leave
surrender your control
and grieve

BOUNDLESS

boundless are your seas
and limitless are your depths
countless are the memories
birthing all the deaths

empty and calm is your mind
and still are your chants
watered evenly is your soil
quenched are your plants

a guardian of the light
and a creature of the dark
there is a mind out there
in need of a spark

so when you enter this unknown
know you are no stranger to the waves
in the midst of a memory
a heart that craves

to be more than what it is and less of what it's not
you long to leave
surrender your control
and grieve

CURRENTCY

you sing of milk and honey
but what of liquid money
that's thick as bible pages
and spineless as loose leafs
in autumn

if you want truth i got em
shackled in the basement of my
abandoned home where sentences roam
like 5G judges and jurors paid under the table
where scraps are scrapped like knees
you want reason i want pleas
you want order i want peace
you want rent i want keys
you want pain i want ease
you want fees i want out

i'm no writer just a dirty water spout
like pork chops frying in grease that
i use to slick back my hair
how heavy your despair
and how light your remorse
full course of libraries turned liars
hear the whispers in the wires
the screeching in the tires
the desperation
yes. we're tired.

CURRENTCY

you sing of milk and honey
but what of liquid money
that's thick as bible pages
and spineless as loose leafs
in autumn

if you want truth i got em
shackled in the basement of my
abandoned home where sentences roam
like 5G judges and jurors paid under the table
where scraps are scrapped like knees
you want reason ~~the~~ i want pleas
you want order i want peace
you want rent i want keys
you want pain i want ease
you want fees i want out

i'm no writer just a dirty water spout
like pork chops frying in grease that
i use to slick back my hair
how heavy your despair
and how light your remorse
full course of libraries turned liars
hear the whispers in the wires
the screeching in the tires
the desperation
yes, we're tired.

As I Am

i am not the light
i am a mirror of the source
so i shall not boast of my luminescence
nor shall i self-proclaim my force
for i am only a vessel to power
i in of myself am not powerful
to confuse being the container
for being what it contains
would be foolish
and i having been a fool
do not seek a cycle of foolishness
nor do i seek a cycle of cycles
for to seek is to desire
and to desire is to pursue
and to pursue is to feel a lack of something
and i do not lack
for i am complete
as i am

As I Am

i am not the light
i am a mirror of the source
so i shall not boast of my luminescence
nor shall i self-proclaim my force
for i am only a vessel to power
i in of myself am not powerful
to confuse being the container
for being what it contains
would be foolish
and i having been a fool
do not seek a cycle of foolishness
nor do i seek a cycle of cycles
for to seek is to desire
and to desire is to pursue
and to pursue is to feel a lack of something
and i do not lack
for i am complete
as i am

SACRA

ailment of alignment continuous confinement
slither syllables non-refillable upon distracting discourse

to be silenced is to be killed while your heart beats
to be silenced is to forget the rhythm of ancestral drums
tantric touch to healing hums

it took a village for you to be here
it took sacrifice for you to take this life for granted
it took blood that watered the roots when there was no water
it took heartbreak, guidance, and hope for you to breathe
it took pressure in the air for your rivers to flow full
it took storms to make your roots expand
it took everything a life could give for you to live
it took and still takes:
quiet sacrifice
stories sealed in coffins
cycles repeated until someone gets it right

you can't see this but i hope
that one day you do
may peace be with you
my friend, my brother, my sister

SACRA

ailment of alignment continuous confinement
slither syllables non-refillable upon distracting discourse

to be silenced is to be killed while your heart beats
to be silenced is to forget the rhythm of ancestral dreams
tantric touch to healing hums

it took a village for you to be here
it took sacrifice for you to take this life for granted
it took blood that watered the roots when there was no water
it took heartbreak, guidance, and hope for you to breathe
it took pressure in the air for your rivers to flow full
it took storms to make your roots expand
it took everything a life could give for you to live
it took and still takes:
quiet sacrifice
stories sealed in coffins
cycles repeated until someone gets it right

you can't see this but i hope
that one day you do
may peace be with you
my friend, my brother, my sister

To Witness

i have witnessed death and
it has witnessed me
time is an illusion
that we can see

our bodies have been viewed as capital
for centuries
we're required to be obedient
digest delusion is
the ingredient inevitable

conditioned to ignore intuition
the fake fruits of fruition fool you into
bodies that rebel for position
push penitentiaries
can you sign this petition?

these c e os' know the damage done
eclipse the sun willful ignorance
when it's said and done
it's them that run

they need us
not the other way around

To Witness

i have witnessed death and
it has witnessed me
time is an illusion
that we can see

our bodies have been viewed as capital
for centuries
we required to be obedient
digest delusion is
the ingredient inevitable

conditioned to ignore intuition
the fake fruits of fruition fool you into
bodies that rebel for position
push penitentiaries
can you sign this petition?

the c e os' know the damage done
eclipse the sun willful ignorance
when it's said and done
it's them that run

they need us
not the other way around

T-Shirt

from car washes with a face you barely knew on a t-shirt
to gofundmes', barbecues, and cheap dirt
black clothes from 2nd hands to be returned by morning
prideful tongues never find mourning

we came together like
prayer hands in times of suffering
AOL speeds so forgive the buffering but
this is the only thing that brings us together

the funerals hurry
with a bottle and worry
to cremate to bury?
to lament the fury
or cement it?

T-Shirt

from car washes with a face you barely knew on a t-shirt
to gofundmes', barbecues, and cheap dirt
black clothes from 2nd hands to be returned by morning
prideful tongues never find mourning

We came together like
prayer hands in times of suffering
AOL speeds so forgive the buffering but
this is the only thing that brings us together

the funerals hurry
with a bottle and worry
to cremate to bury?
to lament the fury
or cement it?

ON THE RUN

laying in my father's arms while he weeps
police sirens and light sleeps
a cracked windshield and cheap hotels
the smell of cigarettes that can't be washed from
the dark shades above the AC that yells

missed calls from my mom crying
the caravan gets lighter the pawn shops are buying
crossing state lines my dad can't walk in straight lines
meeting strangers cd changers fight or flight re-arranger

rest-stops restless paranoia points
i feel the shakiness in my joints
especially my knees
(i'm glad they don't shake like that anymore)
i feel some ease
but still
i can't sleep in cars anymore
i can't run out of gas anymore
i can't remember much of it anymore

ON THE RUN

laying in my father's arms while he weeps
police sirens and light sleeps
a crack windshield and cheap hotels
the smell of cigarettes that can't be washed from
the dark shades above the AC that yells

missed calls from my mom crying
the caravan gets lighter the pawn shops are buying
crossing stat lines my dad can't walk in straight lines
meeting strangers cd changers fight or flight re-arranger

rest-stops restless paranoia points
i feel the shakiness in my joints
especially my knees
(i'm glad they don't shake like that anymore)
i feel some ease
but still
i can't sleep in cars anymore
i can't run out of gas anymore
i can't remember much of it anymore

THE SHACKLED

contrary to consensus
loneliness has loved me
and showed me solitude was a refuge
from uncle to nephew
rusty mossy chains once glossy
not snitching and look where that got me?
break the brackets off of our brains
seize the shackles of letters in names
a language born of blood has slave syllables
slang that hangs from the tongue refillables
so i double cross my heart and hope to die
in the blood of Jesus in the reddest sky
hear me eulogize my thesis
from chapped lips and kitchen puzzle pieces
there's always something missing
memories mark a shifting
snakes aren't always hissing
and shame isn't always sifting

THE SHACKLED

contrary to consensus
lonliness has loved me
and showed me solitude was a refuge
from uncle to nephew
rusty mossy chains once glossy
not snitching and look where that got me?
break the brackets off of our brains
seize the shackles of letters in names
a language born of blood has slave syllables
slang that hangs from the tongue refillables
so i double cross my heart and hope to die
in the blood of Jesus in the reddest sky
hear me eulogize my thesis
from chapped lips and kitchen puzzle pieces
there's always something missing
memories mark a shifting
snakes aren't always hissing
and shame isn't always sifting

YHWH SINGS

YHWH sings to me in synchronicities
with a vowelless language in constant consonants
they say i am the sea and the sun
the truth seeking son
but i say i am the I AM

tainted by painted humanness
the light within lives luminous
with gargoyles at the guardian's gates
evolve evolve
i am the planet's gravitational
revolve resolve
rotation receives motion
poisonous pretty potions
healing hexes in these hazardous lands
with nazareth hands i'm
alchemizing these lazarus sands

power it's what you're after
you've sacrificed your joy and laughter
to get here
but fear
is your master
as a result your death will come faster

YHWH SINGS

YHWH sings to me in synchronicities
with a vowelless language in constant consonants
they say i am the sed and the sun
the truth seeking son
but i say i am the I AM

tainted by humanness
the light within lives luminous
with gargoyles at the guardian's gates
evolve evolve
i am the planet's gravitational
revolve resolve
rotation receives motion
poisonous pretty potions
healing hexes in these hazardous lands
with nazareth hands i'm
alchemizing these Lazarus sands

power is what you're after
you've sacrificed your joy and laughter
to get here
but fear
is your master
as a result your death will come faster

A VOICE

you have a voice
that spoke in the beginning
and a voice that has spoken of my end
i will not plead or pretend
that i do not know your
strength

i will not meander
or mention the length of reach
the tendency to teach that
you summon
for i am a shadow's silhouette
secretly sitting in this sun burnt terrain

i am
the lost traveler's pandering pain
mourning mountains who died in vain
from breaking backs burned by flames
know the names. . .

because you have a voice
a voice like no other
a voice of a mother
a voice of a brother
a voice that speaks in dance

A VOICE

you have a voice
that spoke in the beginning
and a voice that has spoken of my end
i will not plead or pretend
that i do not know your
strength

i will not meander
or mention the length of reach
the tendency to teach that
you summon
for i am a shadow's silhouette
secretly sitting in this sun burnt terrain

i am
the lost traveler's pondering pain
mourning mountains who died in vain
from breaking backs burned by flames
know the names...

because you have a voice
a voice like no other
a voice of a mother
a voice of a brother
a voice that speaks in dance

BARREN BODY

this one is for the days that i can't get outta bed

i wither weather in hopes that it gets better
i leave my friends on read
the days where i feel dread
dead daisies over graves
cause i overgave
this barren body

send shivers down to shifting faces
spiral viral vexes turn to horrid hurtful hexes

open cases with broken laces with hopeful hands
truth be told ima hopeful man in these hopeless lands

i hope you understand
how healing something broken is
very far from what drinkin' n' smokin' is
i don't have the answers but what i'm hopin' is
we can figure out what healthy coping is

this one is for the days i need a life-line
this hurt is heartbreak for a lifetime. . .

BARREN BODY

this one is for the days that i can't get outta bed

i wither weather in hopes that it gets better
i leave my friends on read
the days where i feel dread
dead daisies over graves
cause i overgave
this barren body

send shivers down to shifting faces
spiral viral vexes turn to horrid hurtful hexes

open cases with broken laces with hopeful hands
truth be told ima hopeful man in these hopeless lands

i hope you understand
how healing something broken is
very far from what drinkin' n' smokin' is
i don't have the answers but what i'm hopin' is
we can figure out what healthy coping is

this one is for the days i need a life-line
this hurt is heartbreak for a lifetime

NOPALES

sundials, eggs, and cactus
quiet lips practice
preaching parables
of the sower
the leaf blower
the lawn mower
i push three times a week
to have dead white men over
and under the table
the foreign fable
not able
to roll an R
the hidden scar
hopes to be witnessed
but never is

you see it's cuz these
ancient yoga stacks
hieroglyphs and almanacs
dice rolling col-de-sacs
rolled ankles and broken backs

coded language loaded languish
co-dead language burning anguish
feed the flame you need a name
you'll never know but
you'll know the shame

NOPALES

sundials, eggs, and cactus
quiet lips practice
preaching parables
of the sower
the leaf blower
the lawn mower
i push three times a week
to have dead white men over
and under the table
the foreign fable
not able
to roll an R
the hidden scar
hopes to be witnessed
but never is

you see its cause these
ancient yoga stacks
hieroglyphs and almanacs
dice rolling col de sacs in sac
rolled ankles and broken backs

coded language loaded languish
co-dead language burning anguish
feed the flame you need a name
you'll never know but
you'll know the shame

Buzzin'

another thinker turned drinker
a blonde blushing blinker cracked from concrete
the world wonders why the addict on-heat hook line sinkers
as if vines don't grow melons with melancholy
everything is connected the train the trolly
intersected by the street's veins
the graffiti the foley the rolie
mystic mania of re-enacting wrestle-mania wholly
with cousins buzzin' like buzzer beaters
i seen men control and beat her — so —
another swig to break the twig of bone
pawn shops go and sell what you own
belongings: a backpack and a metro pc phone
hate thy reflection
how great thy projection
of passive pacifists how about
you pass a fist of boxing gloves?
gloating before you know it
with the scars to show it
haymakers from fake leather the color of red plastic cups
to the edge of the top story where there's no more looking up
so broken we become breaking news
looking down at people making blues
to your pain that you'll paint on the sidewalk
the city chants always drown me out
so i don't even know why i talk

BUZZIN'

another thinker turned drinker
a blonde blushing blinker cracked from concrete
the world wonders why the addict on heat hook line sinkers
as if vines don't grow melons with melancholy
everything is connected the train the trolly
intersected by the street's veins
the graffiti the foley the rolie
mystic mania of re-enacting wrestle-mania wholly
with cousins buzzin' like buzzer beaters
i seen men control and beat her — so —
another swig to break the twig of bone
pawn shops go and sell what you own
belongings: a backpack and a metro pc phone
hate thy reflection
how great thy projection
of passive pacifists how about
you pass a fist of boxing gloves?
gloating before you knew it
with the scars to show it
haymakers from fake leather the color of red plastic cups
to the edge of the top story where there's no more looking up
so broken we become breaking news
looking down at people making blues
to your pain that you'll paint on the sidewalk
the city chants always drown me out
so i don't even know why i talk

113

QUARREL

the force of god in reverse
rehearsed like a lie that sounds like truth
youthful eulogies you'd be a fool full of seas
stormy stars with flashing fading scars drowning by
the putrid bars that laws are made for safety and morals
cut my chords on corals to finish me and drown my quiet quarrels

the laughing law is the whip and ignorance is the ship
set sail to the arrogance that prevails in punishing fashion
i wear clothes from thrift stores too poor to be more so i drive for
a four door and wear hand me downs
for four wars in seven days
exhale eleven ways
you take or you're taken
by your own god you in-hail the shaken
salt to snails hails of heavenly horrors
the torture is that dying is less expensive for me

more importantly
as i see this world distortedly
my bedroom blankets are the only ones that feel me rest
the only warmth to compress coldness in this throbbing chest
like the crushed ice that clinks against the glass
and the rain that patters against the window pass
the air is toxic with my tendencies of torn tendons ripped tenderly
aching baffled the haunting scaffold will you render me?

QUARREL

the force of god in reverse
rehearsed like a lie that sounds like truth
youthful eulogies you'd be a fool full of seas
stormy stars with flashing fading scars drowning by
the putrid bars that laws are made for safety and morals
cut my chords on corals to finish me and drown my quiet quarrels

the laughing law is the whip and ignorance is the ship
set sail to the arrogance that prevails in punishing fashion
i wear clothes from thrift stores too poor to be more so i drive for
a four door and wear hand me downs
for four wars in seven days
exhale eleven ways
you take or you're taken
by your own god yey in-hail the shaken
salt to snails hails of heavenly horrors
the torture is that dying is less expensive for me

more importantly
as i see this world distortedly
my bedroom blankets are the only ones that feel me rest
the only warmth to compress coldness in this throbbing chest
like the crushed ice that clinks against the glass
and the rain that patters against the window pass
the air is toxic with my tendencies of torn tendons ripped tenderly
aching baffled ~~by the ever~~ haunting scaffold will you ~~tender~~ me?

FIGS

i was three words too early
and a heartbreak too late
with the foresight of my altar
i had to alter state

reality was too rude
dancing with my death was too crude
an inescapable facing of self
i reeked
of an unchecked ego

being prideful emptied me
being selfless was fulfilling
living in my surface world confused me
and going inward was revealing

i had to live with disgust
and distrust of my perceptions
the smoking mirrors of my fears
deepened my deceptions

the taste notes of rotting fig corpses
malted jasmine and grapefruit that was too acidic to stomach
the grinds whisper to me at the bottom of the mug
the aroma of warmth in the cold light leaks
the capturing of a moving moment on 35mm
the stillness the realization that no choice is a choice

116

FIGS

i was three words too early
and a heartbreak too late
with the foresight of my altar
i had to alter state

reality was too rude
dancing with my death was too crude
an inescapable facing of self
i reeked
of an unchecked ego

being prideful emptied me
being selfless was fulfilling
living in my surface world confused me
and going inward was revealing

i had to live with disgust
and distrust of my perceptions
the smoking mirrors of my fears
deepened my deceptions

the taste notes of rotting fig corpses
malted a jasmine and grapefruit that was too acidic to stomach
the grinds whisper to me at the bottom of the mug
the aroma of warmth in the cold light leaks
the capturing of a moving moment on 35mm
the stillness the realization that no choice is a choice

117

Oм

black cat, white rabbit, deer with branches for antlers
speak in spray paint, sharpies, and house pot planters

food for fishes
dirty dishes in the sink
wounds with wishes
sounds of swishes
a thought to think

emptiness reflected
fullness expected
running from stillness
wellness illness

self-castigation
self-annihilation
a yearning for the years to slow down
food or water no longer goes down
even with gravity's help
i am kelp
for bottom feeders
welts on my eyes from walgreen readers
hit for being nosey i'm in the nose bleeders
in a wife beater with red splotches
i've been drowning in my failures
ears ringing from the notches
shaking from the anxiousness
watching the melting watches

Oм

black cat, white rabbit, deer with branches for antlers
speak in spray paint, sharpies, and house pot planters

food for fishes
dirty dishes in the sink
wounds with wishes
sounds of swishes
a thought to think

emptiness reflected
fullness expected
running from stillness
wellness illness

self-castigation
self-annihilation
a yearning for the years to slow down
food or water no longer goes down
even with gravity's help
i am kelp
for bottom feeders
welts on my eyes from walgreen readers
hit for being nosey i'm in the nose bleeders
in a wife beater with red splotches
i've been drowning in my failures
ears ringing from the ~~crooked~~ notches
shaking from the anxiousness
watching the melting watches

MOLD ON THE FRUITS

my family is fucked up. plague touched the roots the branches the leaves. no one grieves. everyone leaves. the rotting flowers held by mildew sleeves. white speckles like freckles on the bark. true colors come out the dark. with eyes hollow. lies swallow. the truth when you find out they got touched and who did it.

it's easier to peel the flesh then say there's mold on the fruit. wicked deeds done making tongues mute. parasitic purity—plastic intention. fear-induced abstention. i got preyed on when i needed a prayer the most. when i needed a father the most. when i needed someone, anyone. a youth pastor got too close. to where i forgot. what actually happened and what did not. now i can't trust myself. now i can't trust no man. i fought. and fight. to understand. why it keeps coming up. man

i'm fucked up cause i come from a broken home. lice in the comb. scars on the dome. only seen my mom and dad hug once. home. in my memories i'm alone. they cursed the phone. alone. my pops in n' out of a cell (now he's dead) oh well. my mom wasn't feeling well (she always said). my sleepwalking and sleeptalking may be hell (feeling dread) do i need jesus? it's hard to tell — you

i'm fucked up. even after the therapy even after the acid i have these flashbacks screaming rancid who need attention. the weight i bare is too much to mention. it compresses my spirit and stretches my soul. into dimensions i never feel whole. i want to die so is living the goal? i'm fucked up but these medi-cal therapists say i'm fine. i tell myself the same thing even though i know i'm lyin'

MOLD ON THE FRUITS

my family is fucked up. plague touched the roots the branches the leaves. no one grieves. everyone leaves. the rotting flowers held by mildew sleeves. white speckles like freckles on the bark. true colors come out the dark. with eyes hollow. lies swallow. the truth when you find out they got touched and who did it.

it's easier to peel the flesh then say there's mold on the fruit. wicked deeds done making tongues mute. parasitic purity – plastic intentions fear-induced abstention. i got preyed on when i needed a prayer the most. when i needed a father the most. when i needed someone, anyone the most. a youth pastor got too close. to where i forgot. what actually happened and what did not. now i can't trust myself. now i can't trust no men. i fought. and fight. to understand. why it keeps coming up. man

i'm fucked up cause i come from a broken home. lice in the comb. scars on the dome. only seen my mom and dad hug once. home. in my memories i'm alone. they cursed the phone. alone. my pops in n'out of a cell (now he's dead) oh well. my mom wasn't feeling well (she always said). my sleepwalking and sleeptalking may be hell (feeling dread) do i need jesus? its hard to tell — you

i'm fucked up. even after the therapy even after the acid i have these flashbacks screaming rancid who need attention. the weight i bare is too much to mention. it compresses my spirit and stretches my soul. into dimensions i never feel whole. i want to die so is living the goal? i'm fucked up but these medi-cal therapists say i'm fine. i tell myself the same thing even though i know i'm lyin'

iv. freedom costs

seeking freedom feels like
an imprisoning process in itself

FREEDOM COSTS

born in 95 doing 9 to 5s
the sweetness is that of honey hives
or money i've
placed in mason jars
adjacent scars from chasing cars
with broken windshields with wipers like vipers

squeeze a penny from my dollar to snipers
in towers i'm paid by the hour a cent of my time
a sense of delusion
it's no wonder i'm

gated as heaven
is that eleven or snake eyes?
your words cut like steak knives
two tongues too tongue tied to take tithes

what an imaginary feeling
staring at my ceiling
abstract: a 4 word contract
to reminisce a kiss of amethyst
with fist
to cheek
to turn
to speak
of elephants as elegant in their size
suffering in silence solemnly wise
denouncing my deity until it dies

FREEDOM COSTS

born in 95 doing 9 to 5s
the sweetness is that of honey hives
or money i've
placed in mason jars
adjacent scars from chasing cars
with broken windshields with wipers like vipers

squeeze a penny from my dollar to snipers
in towers i'm paid by the hour a cent of my time
a sense of delusion
it's no wonder i'm

gated as heaven
is that eleven or snake eyes?
your words cut like steak knives
two tongues too tongue tied to take tithes

what an imaginary feeling
staring at my ceiling
abstracts a 4 word contract
to reminisce a kiss of amethyst
with fist
to cheek
to turn
to speak
of elephants as elegant in their size
suffering in silence solemnly wise
denouncing my deity until it dies

HALF-CAFF

i work amongst the patagonia puffers
the barefoot boys
the teslas
buffered
the bicycles electric
the coffee eclectic
the six dollar lattes
the foam of hokas like cappuccinos
a non-single origin half-caff
laboring latino
an invention
light, medium, and dark roasted calloused hands
that pray for ascension
i don't want to eat in rations
renting myself to pay for passions
getting nostalgic for processed food
serving those entitled, unaware, and rude
i can't afford the coffee i make
i can't afford the pastries i bake
that i take
when they're day olds
i'm bound to how the day folds, me up
like a compostable cup
only to throw me in the trash
return me to the ash
we all end up in the landfill anyways
you don't care that the land feels many ways

HALF-CAFE

i work amongst the patagonia puffers
the barefoot boys
the teslas
buffered
the bicycles electric
the coffee eclectic
the six dollar lattes
the foam of hokas like cappuccinos
a non-single origin half-caff
laboring latino
an invention
light, medium, and dark roasted calloused hands
that pray for ascension
i don't want to eat in rations
renting myself to pay for passions
getting nostalgic for processed food
serving those entitled, unaware, and rude
i can't afford the coffee i make
i can't afford the pastries i bake
that i take
when they're day olds
i'm bound to how the day folds, me up
like a compostable cup
only to throw me in the trash
return me to the ash
we all end up in the landfill any ways
you don't care that the land feels many ways

CAPITAL W/SOME ISM

life feels uphill when you
have to pay the bills
month to month survival
you know how this kills
you slowly

the nauseating feeling of going to work at places
where we're replaceable and expendable
where we're pressured to be dependable
where we need to have an open schedule
and a closed mind

my value in this country is dependent on
how much i contribute to the machine
how much i uphold someones else's dream
and that for me is not poetic
it's depressing as fuck

CAPITAL W/SOME ISM

life feels uphill when you
have to pay the bills
month to month survival
you know how this kills
you slowly

the nauseating feeling of going to work at places
where where we're replaceable and expendable
where wo're pressured to be dependable
where we need to have an open schedule
and a closed mind

my value in this country is dependent on
how much i contribute to the machine
how much i uphold someone else's dream
and that for me is not poetic
its depressing as fuck

129

CRACKED

cracked mortar
dissembling disorders
what are your requirements
to see without borders

chess pieces with chokers
river sounds with smokers
two opposing pieces
playground recess
i felt free
nose diving in books
till the sun rose
only to die with hook in mouth to nose
how love goes south
in a matter of minutes
moments memories
you know
one word has a way
of bulldozing a foundation
that was built by enemies
twisted by the imbalance
defused by the valance
do you have the spine?
do you have the stomach?
do you have the heart?
the courage to be more
than their words?

CRACKED

cracked mortar
dissembling disorders
what are your requirements
to see without borders

chess pieces with chokers
river sounds with smokers
two opposing pieces
playground recess
i felt free
nose diving in books
till the sun rose
only to die with hook in mouth to nose
how love goes south
in a matter of minutes
moments memories
you know
one word has a way
of bulldozing a foundation
that was built by enemies
twisted by the imbalance
defused by the valance
do you have the spine?
do you have the stomach?
do you have the heart?
the courage to be more
than their words?

G.M.Owed

warped, ultra-processed, and modified
is the ego of this wretched realm
the water is corrupted static
detached from source so
coarse is the skin's remorse that has grown thick
polluted is my stomach that has grown sick
and sour of the parables that tower tastelessly

inflamed with abuse
in flames is my muse
exhale the excuse
in hail because
as i said before
you're your own
god

in the land of the shackles the corporate cackles
remind us that resistance is a state of being
not some trend to be posted then deleted
virtue signaling rinsed and repeated
steep the tea that your body needs
peep the people that plot in the shadows of weeds
beware of the ego deaths and the delirium
the false prophets, the propped up leaders, to the fools
they will try to disarm you with their schools
whats my advice? the smarter your tools
the dumber you get

G.M.Owed

Warped, ultra-processed, and modified
is the ego of this wretched realm
the water is corrupted static
detached from source so
coarse is the skin's remorse that has grown thick
polluted is my stomach that has grown sick
and sour of the parables that tower tastelessly.

inflamed with abuse
in flames is my muse
exhale the excuse
in hail because
as i said before
you're your own
god

in the land of the shackles, the corporate cackles
remind us that resistance is a state of being
not some trend to be posted then deleted
virtue signaling rinsed and repeated
steep the tea that your body needs
peep the people that plot in the shadows of weeds
beware of the ego deaths and the delirium
the false prophets, the propped up leaders, to the fools
they will try to disarm you with their schools
whats my advice? the smarter your tools
the dumber you get

133

Maggot

i wish i could say
i went from caterpillar to butterfly
but truth be told its been maggot to fly
i was thrown in the garbage to die
i ate all the shit people gave me
and now it's fuck them
cause now
i can fly

It Always Comes Back

it's scratching it's clawing
gnawing on my pores and pupils
incisors on my cuticles
although this is my usual i want it to stop
it holds me scolds me
folds me into shapes i hate
makes me regurgitate nonstop
it comes. it goes. and always has to feed on me
taking more than what it needs from me
i can't escape
my skin crawling
more and more as days go by
when it's calling i lay awake and wonder why
i've fallen into this fashion where i feel i can't say no
it always over takes its ration
i'm tired… and it shows

MAGGOT

i wish i could say
i went from caterpillar to butterfly
but truth be told its been maggot to fly
i was thrown in the garbage to die
i ate all the shit people gave me
and now it's fuck them
cause now
i can fly

IT ALWAYS COMES BACK

it's scratching it's clawing
gnawing on my pores and pupils
incisors on my cuticles
although this is my usual i want it to stop
it holds me scolds me
folds me into shapes i hate
makes me regurgitate nonstop
it comes it goes and always has to feed on me
taking more than what it needs from me
i can't escape
my skin crawling
more and more as days go by
when it's calling i lay awake and wonder why
i've fallen into this fashion where i feel i can't say no
it always over takes its ration
i'm tired... and it shows

MERCURY

searching for balance through tasting tolerance
teasing my tastebuds of a tasteless ceasefire
a facade foolish as fools gold
too old to think young
and too young to know
how nothing can stay
not a smile or day
all things end
don't befriend
a habitat hazed in teenage smoke
drinks poured like Seattle rain
snakes sliding under jokes
hands breaking boundaries against foreign terrain
collecting bodies becoming hoarders
disdained is the distant tongue licking borders
too juxtaposed to hear the origin
of a near embrace
seeking a solace you call home
but home is gone and wrapped in foam
a concrete crumble on the news
a memory to carry in silent dues
violent views
torturous steps
not taken by
most

MERCURY

searching for balance through tasting tolerance
teasing my taste buds of a tasteless ceasefire
a facade foolish as fools gold
too old to think young
and too young to know
how nothing can stay
not a smile or day
all things end
don't befriend
a habitat hazed in teenage smoke
drinks poured like Seattle rain
snakes sliding under jokes
hands breaking boundaries against foreign terrain
collecting bodies becoming hoarders
disdained is the distant tongue licking borders
too juxtaposed to hear the origin
of a near embrace
seeking a solace you call home
but home is gone and wrapped in foam
a concrete crumble on the news
a memory to carry in silent dues
violent views
torturous steps
not taken by
most

ITERATIONS

i'm a mood shifter
a mood lifter hypervigilant and ever-changing
i'm whoever you need me to be rearranging
sets of illusions an actor whatever the part
my function is to alter shape to alter heart

i change form i change tone
i'm witnessed then unknown
all that is
all that can be
all the parts of family
i don't talk to

from white tees going past my waist line
and the belts holding jeans too big
to reanimating my face
reincarnated
dig

deeper for what it is i seek
intentions reek
when not aligned
with my physique
dig

deeper to bitter truths
and better roots

ITERATIONS

i'm a mood shifter
a mood lifter hypervigilant and ever-changing
i'm whoever you need me to be rearranging
sets of illusions an actor whatever the part
my function is to alter shape to alter heart

i change form i change tone
i'm witnessed then unknown
all that is
all that can be
all the parts of family
i don't talk to

from white tees going past my waist line
and the belts holding jeans too big
to reanimating my face
reincarnated
dig

deeper for what it is i seek
intentions reek
when not aligned
with my physique
dig
~~deeper~~
deeper to bitter truths
and better roots

FREEDOM WITH A COST

a part of me has died today
a part of me is gone
day by day and week by week
there's no use in going on.

for this system is not made
for a free soul like me
incarceration or suicide
seem likely.

money has no interest
to a body that has no hope
time has no interest when
i've found no way to cope.

FREEDOM WITH A COST

a part of me has died today
a part of me is gone
day by day and week by week
there's no use in going on.

for this system is not made
for a free soul like me
incarcerated or suicide
seem likely.

money has no interest
to a body that has no hope
time has no interest when
i've found no way to cope.

THAT HUG

months on end
without having a long embrace
they see my face
and think
i get so much touch
sex is my crutch
to the deeper pain of not being held
by others
isolation i'm missing deep intimacy
a back rub a back scratched feet rubbed
index and middle finger tracing my outlines
holding another whose shape forms to mines
and mine to theirs
i've had this and yet had to leave stares
where admiration filled the iris
i'm no good for anyone
because i know everything
comes to an end
and that truth kills a forever
so
i go from body to body
cause i can only be held and hold with sex
but even then i feel the deeper wound in the after
of the sweat of love making or bodies needing friction
it's fiction faking itself to be how love actually incarnates
you just met me and gave me this long hug and i really needed that,
so i wanted to say thank you

THAT HUG

months on end
without having a long embrace
they see my face
and think
i get so much touch
sex is my crutch
to the deeper pain of not being held
by others
isolation i'm missing deep intimacy
a back rub a back scratched feet rubbed
index and middle finger tracing my outlines
holding another whose shape forms to mines
and mine to theirs
i've had this and yet had to leave stares
where admiration filled the iris
i'm no good for anyone
because i know everything
comes to an end
and that truth kills a forever
so
i go from body to body
cause i can only be held and hold with sex
but even then i feel the deeper wound in the after
of the sweat of love making or bodies needing friction
it's fiction faking itself to be how love actually incarnates
you just met me and gave me this long hug and i really needed that,
so i wanted to say thank you

THESIS

this is my faster thesis
i broke my heart into masterpieces
masterful servitude with fractured leases
you see veins but i see roots to the heart
a network flowing in elegance
spewing art
of arteries
with razor blades accurate
as archeries
what then
is truth spilt for?
false prophets all for profits
draining validation down our faucets
of forgotten jigsawed joints out of sockets
pressurized and formed to lockets
blasting rockets from stolen picked pockets
propping spineless book corpses with scorched pages
contrary to you and sages
i like how your
mood swing swings misses
how your
mood sing sings kisses
how you're like boiling water hisses
burnt tongue tips and
dying rose hips
to pose lips

THESIS

this is my faster thesis
i broke my heart into masterpieces
masterful servitude with fractured leases
you see veins but i see roots to the heart
a network flowing in elegance
spewing art
of arteries
with razor blades accurate
as archeries
what then
is truth spilt for?
false prophets all for profits
draining validation down our faucets
of forgotten jigsawed joints of sockets
pressurized and formed to lockets
blasting rockets from stolen picked pockets
propping spineless book corpses with scorched pages
contrary to you and sages
i like how your
mood swing swings misses
how your boiling water hisses
burnt tongue tips and
dying rose hips
to poor lips

RIPPLES

water color ripples that
pulsate like portals
peaches in pieces
with snippets of conversation

they change with the touch
for every reaction there is a
raised hand craving bruised skin
the child within

when you need a shield
the artist is revealed
or you die slowly from others
or quickly by your hands

i am
you are
energetically aware of ourselves
creating chaos just to feel our expansion

i am
you are
becoming
no more running
no more chasing
just attracting
reflecting and facing

RIPPLES

water color ripples that
pulsate like portals
peaches in pieces
with snippets of conversation

they change with the touch
for every reaction there is a
raised hand craving bruised skin
the child within

when you need a shield
the artist is revealed
or #you die slowly from others
or quickly by your hands

i am
you are
energetically aware of ourselves
creating chaos just to feel our expansion

i am
you are
becoming
no more running
no more chasing
just attracting
reflecting and facing

FADE AWAY

i watch myself fade away into
wrinkles and bald spots.
the street lights flicker
on talking shoes parking lots.

the highs have stopped feeling so high
and the lows never seem to find the floor.
why is that the things that i dread
never find a door?

it feels pointless
to go on living as everyone you love, dies.
you see your face reflected in their
dissociated eyes.

i could never know what it's like
to be you.
i only know what it's like
to be see through.

148

FADE AWAY

i watch myself fade into
wrinkles and bald spots.
the street lights flicker
on talking shoes parking lots.

the highs have stopped feeling so high
and the lows never seem to find the floor.
why is it that the things that i dread
never find a door?

it feels pointless
to go on living as everyone you love, dies.
you see your face reflected in their
dissociated eyes.

i could never know what it's like
to ~~be you~~ see you.
i only know what it's like
to be see through.

How

how do i radically love myself
when indifference is all i feel?
is it my responsibility to heal?
to change my heart?
to break the generational chains?
to sacrifice my safety for the creating of art?

my soul in soil
processing through portals
staring into something mid-prayer
mountains, morals, mundane mortals

in this sea i've known
an empty container praying to no god
too spiritually damaged and
carelessly overgrown
like the ivy on our home
the sunbleached gnome
broken windows and squatters
candy wrappers and plastic waters
bottled up with anger
of flesh and metal hangers
don't talk to strangers
except my parents
one remains

HOW

how do i radically love myself
when indifference is all i feel?
is it my responsibility to heal?
to change my heart?
to break the generational chains?
to sacrifice my safety for the creating of art?

my soul in soil
processing through portals
staring into something mid-prayer
mountains, morals, mundane mortals

in this sea i've known
an empty container praying to no god
too spiritually damaged and
carelessly overgrown
like the ivy on our home
the sunbleached gnome
broken windows and squatters
candy wrappers and plastic waters
bottled up with anger
of flesh and metal hangers
don't talk to strangers
except my parents
one remains

151

Plastic Bags

a face the sun hasn't kissed
a face forgotten by the mist
add another tally to the wrist
you get the gist

shower shimmer glitter glimmer
kisses on my sternum
love notes i burn em
grave soil i turn em

poised in perfection
a poison reflection of you
horizon with sun risin'
how pretty the hue

plastic bags as tumbleweeds
heat stings like bumblebees

PLASTIC BAGS

a face the sun hasn't kissed
a face forgotten by the mist
add another tally to the wrist
you get the gist

shower shimmer glitter glimmer
kisses on my sternum
love notes i burn em
grave soil i turn em

poised in perfection
a poison reflection of you
horizon with sun risin'
how pretty the hue

plastic bags as tumbleweeds
heat stings like bumblebees

153

You will never know

you will never know love until
  you kiss the earth that birthed you.

you will never know forgiveness until
  you forgive the tongue that cursed you.

you will never know yourself until
  you hold the hand that hurt you.

you will never know.

Alive

i'm getting older way too fast.
these moments never seem to last.
i'm usually the one that leaves
but now i am the one that grieves.

who knew
that i'd still be alive today.
you too
i'm glad that you're alive.
i'm glad that you're alive.
i'm glad that you're alive, today.

You Will Never Know

you will never know love until
  you kiss the earth that birthed you.

you will never know forgiveness until
  you forgive the tongue that cursed you.

you will never know yourself until
  you hold the hand that hurt you.

you will never know.

Alive

i'm getting older way too fast.
these moments never seem to last.
i'm usually the one that leaves
but now i am the one that grieves.

who knew.
that i'd still be alive today.
you too
i'm glad that you're alive.
i'm glad that you're alive.
i'm glad that you're alive, today.

A Day At The Beach

empty cans tumbling on the sand
the taste of sea salt blowing on my lips
the echoes of the cave and the dripping mango drips
lager sips with temperature whips
the protruding whisper of the wind
makes my ears ache
the fantasy i had before
is now foolish and fake

my body quivers to warm vibrating shivers
the unfair fahrenheit brings me to this moment

maybe that's why i'm here?
alone and in fear
with no apparent danger
a familiar stranger full of emptiness

i sense grief inside this cove
i sense graves inside this grove
it's the way the fallen rocks lay like tombstones
the sediments of sentiment of crystal in grainy mounds

the way the breeze wheezes, whistles, and swells
footprints to nowhere hands to seashells
i can hear the ocean if i put it closer to my earring
and just like that i'm transported back to my
mom's oceancore bathroom when wonder was all that i was hearing

A Day At The Beach

empty cans tumbling on the sand
the taste of sea salt blowing on my lips
the echoes of the cave and the dripping mango drips
lager sips with temperature whips

the protruding whisper of the wind
makes my ears ache
the fantasy i had before
is now foolish and fake

my body quivers to warm vibrating shivers
the unfair fahrenheit brings me to this moment

maybe that's why i'm here?
alone and in fear
with no apparent danger
a familiar stranger full of emptiness

i sense grief inside this cove
i sense graves inside this grove
it's the way the fallen rocks lay like tombstones
the sediments of sentiment of crystalin grainy mounds

the way the breeze wheezes, whistles, and swells
footprints to nowhere hands to seashells
i can hear the ocean if i put it closer to my earring
and just like that i'm transported back to my
mom's oceancore bathroom when wonder was all that i was hearing

CAFES

the eyes see
a barista with dyed hair, face piercings, and a book with a book-marker
further in the pages then the last time the eyes saw them
the lips smile the teeth peek while the crows feet by the eyes perch
the mouth speaks almost inaudibly from behind the fiberglass
the hand takes a piece of plastic outside of the denim pocket
the plastic is tapped on the display screen
the hand is handed a warm mug with three grapefruits painted on it
the tongue is reminded that it doesn't like grapefruit
the mind reassures the tongue that it's only a painting on some ceramic
the tongue understands this explanation
the mug is then taken to sit on a wooden table that wobbles
the hand puts the mug to lips and the first sip of
a five dollar latte (+ tip) is taken
the mind is reminded that the piece of plastic is
reaching for its limit
the mind is reminded that the hands need
to start working again
but the hands are so stubborn these days
they're burnt out and so they protest
this distresses the mind so
another sip of the five dollar latte (+ tip) is taken

the hands start to write
and remember that it's something they like doing
for a moment the hands begin to work again.
another sip of the five dollar latte (+ tip) is taken. it's gone.

CAFES

the eyes see
a barista with dyed hair, face piercings, and a book with a book-marker
further in the pages then the last time the eyes saw them
the lips smile the teeth peak while the crows feet by the eyes perch
the mouth speaks almost inaudibly from behind the fiberglass
the hand takes a piece of plastic outside of the denim pocket
the plastic is tapped on the display screen
the hand is handed a warm mug with three grapefruits painted on it
the tongue is reminded that it doesn't like grapefruit
the mind reassures the tongue that it's only a painting on some ceramic
the tongue understands this explanation
the mug is then taken to sit on a wooden table that wobbles
the hand puts the mug to lips and the first sip of
a five dollar latte (+ tip) is taken
the mind is reminded that the piece of plastic is
reaching for its limit
the mind is reminded that the hands need
to start working again
but the hands are so stubborn these days
they're burnt out and so they protest
this distresses the mind so
another sip of the five dollar latte (+ tip) is taken

the hands start to write
and remember that it's something they like doing
for a moment the hands begin to work again
another tip of the five dollar latte (+ tip) is taken. now it's gone.

QUESTIONS 4 A CITY

When do you belong to a city?
is it when its cut you and soaked your blood into the asphalt?
is it when you know its backroads, alleyways, and unmarked trails?
is it when you've given your tears? given your years?
give your ears to listen to its soundscape of birds to gun shots?

When are you from a city?
does being born in a place make you from that place?
does having memories everywhere you go make you from there?
or is that not enough?
is it having so many memories stacked on a spatial position that gives
you the right, the blessing, the privilege to say i'm from _____.
When do you belong to a city? because i really wanna know
when i can call a city my home.
is it when the people hold you and you hold them?
is it when people see you and don't look twice because you belong?
is it when you know how to dance the songs? when you
know the ebb and flow. when you know when traffic hits.
when you can tell someone, "eat here. check this out. you'll like this."?
when being in other places only makes you long to be back there?
When?
because i've never felt like i've belonged anywhere no matter
how much: my words change, my body language shifts, my groove
to the backbeat of the city sits. maybe i belong nowhere? or maybe
i do belong "here", wherever here is. there, there.

[Or maybe none of us can ever belong to something that's been stolen?
maybe belonging isn't in the cards for people like me that live in the
inbetween? maybe i'm from nowhere.]

160

QUESTIONS 4 A CITY

When do you belong to a city?
is it when it's cut you and soaked your blood into the asphalt?
is it when you know it's back roads, alleyways, and unmarked trails?
is it when you've given your tears? given your years?
given your ears to listen to it's soundscape of birds to gun shots?

When are you from a city?
does being born within a place make you from that place?   or is that
does having memories everywhere you go make you from there? not enough?
or does having so many memories stack'd on a spatial position that gives
you the right, the blessing, the privledge to say i'm from_____.
When do you belong to a city? because i really wanna know.
When can you call a city home? i can call a city my home.
is it when the people hold you and you hold them?
is it when people see you and don't look twice because you belong?
is it when you know how to dance the songs? When you
know the ebb and flow. when you know when traffic hits.
when you can tell someone, "eat here. check this out. you'll like this."?
when being in other places only makes you long to be back there?
When?
because i've never felt like i've belonged anywhere, no matter
how much: my words change, my body language shifts, my groove
to the back beat of the city's. maybe i belong nowhere. or maybe
i do belong "here", wherever here is. there, there.

Or maybe none of us can ever belong to something that's
been stolen? maybe belonging isn't in the cards for people
like me that live in the inbetween? maybe i'm from nowhere

161

DEATH INSTINCT

my *id* is my I.D.
life support - I.V.
hair long like IVY
victim mindset "WHY ME!?"

i don't think of myself highly
still don't you ever try me
primal ticks ticking timely
down with the ego ideal
i do it idly

SHRED OF DREAD THE DEAD IN MY HEAD

cutting time with a <u>blink</u>
morbid orbit thoughts to <u>think</u>
death <u>instinct</u>
destructive nature
agressive obsessive adolescence
down the drains
up the veins
all in-vain
fall in-rain
the bane
  of [my] existence

DEATH INSTINCT

my id is my I.D.
life support — I.V.
hair long like IVy
victim ~~set mindset~~ why me!?
           screaming
i don't think of my highly
still don't you try me
primal ~~ticks~~ ticking timely
~~ego~~ down with the ego ideal; do it idly

SHred of Dread the dead in my Head

Cutting time with a <u>blink</u>
morbid orbit thoughts to <u>think</u>
death <u>instinct</u>
destructive nature
~~agres~~ agressive obsessive adolescense
down the drain
up the veins
all in-vain
x fall in-sane
caw in-rain
the bane
        of existance

v. crying over spilt beer

we get so busy living
we forget about dying
tell them you love them
and give passage to crying

CRYING OVER SPILT BEER

bottom of the bottle of anxiety. always tryna make it to sobriety. never could fit in society. not really sure why you lied to me.

i idolized you while you idly were out my life until finally you said, "here's my fears, here's my tears, and here's my beer, cheers!"

to another mother that lost her son. to another son that lost his dad. sad that i don't feel bad cause you didn't even see me grad-u-ate i'm glad-you-ain't in my life cause madness makes and sadness takes its toll. till death drink us part yeah you reached your goal on that hospital bed yeah i seen you swole. woah. i seen you go. i cried on you just so you know. reap and sow just know you won't ever even get the chance to see me grow.

and true i loved you but you loved the bottle more and that's when we knew that you were never coming back and that's when your veins went black. . . so leap in faith to find your way

cause tears pour out like spilt beer. you're gone but i'm still here. suicide is still near like a rearview if i listen to the silence i can hear you. if i drink i'm near you. and

if i knew then what i knew now i would have given you that money. nose runny eyes running faster. like father like son a running disaster. so plaster the pastor's tongue on your casket get the henny and jose to mask it. tragic.

CRYING OVER SPILT BEER

bottom of the bottle of anxiety. always tryna make it to sobriety. never
could fit in society. not really sure why you lied to me.

i idolized you. while you idly were out my life until finally you said,
"here's my tears, here's my teats, and here's my beer, cheers."

to another mother that lost her son. to another son that lost his dad. sad
that i don't feel bad cause you didn't even see me grad-u-ate i'm glad-
you ain't in my life cause madness makes and sadness takes its toll. till
death drink us part yeah you reached your goal on that hospital bed
yeah i seen you swole. woah, i seen you go. i cried on you just so you
know. reap and sew just know you won't ever even get the chance to
see me grow.

and true i love you but you loved the bottle more and that's when we
knew that you were never coming back and that's when your veins went
black. so leap in faith to find your way// i'm glad she didn't see
you like that
cause tears pour out like spilt beer. you're gone but i'm still here.
suicide is still near like a rearview. if i listen to the sirens i can hear
you. if i drink i'm near you. and

if i knew then what i knew now i would have given you that money.
now runny eyes running faster. like father like son a running disaster.
so plaster the pastor's tongue on your casket got the hurry and jest to
mask it. tragic.

WHITE WASHED

white washed like uh overexposed film shot
sun was peaked knuckle to the wall like a rim shot
wish it woulda been me i could take his spot
drywall why-call motel go-tell poolside it's hot
haze of the valley heat diss-ease dizzy
belly bent from all the hot honda back seats track meets
tint always peeling brakes always squealing
feelings always fleeting
sega genesis never beating
on to the next next level on to the next next next next devil
what does it matter if it's back to the rubble?
it's
6 feet over always goin under
demons in my headphones soundin' like thunder
in o-k-c with no AC you were in a coma so we went-to-see
the power of a preacher
nowhere in the bleachers abandoned by my teachers
nothing in my shoebox no one left to box
wish i would of told you but we can't talk
ticking time bomb chip on my shoulder sun block
2pac 2years goin' by
never knowin' why
go ahead n' die
why i even try
i—i
actually don't even know

WHITE WASHED

white washed like uh overexposed film shot
sum was peaked knuckle to the wall like a rim shot
wish it woulda been me i could take his spot
drywall why-call motel go-tell poolside it's hot
haze of the valley heat dias-ease dizzy
belly bent from all the hot honda back seats track meets
tint always peeling brakes always squealing
feelings always fleeting
sega genesis never beating
on to the next next level on to the next next next next devil
what does it matter if it's back to the rubble?
it's
6 feet over always goin' under
demons in my headphones soundin' like thunder
in o-k-c with no AC you were in a coma so we went-to-see
the power of a preacher
nowhere in the bleachers abandoned by my teachers
nothing in my shoe box no one left to box
wish i would of told you but we can't talk
ticking time bomb chip on my shoulder sun block
2pac 2 years goin' by
never knowin' why
go ahead n' die
why i even try
i—i
actually don't even know

SPLIT

i'm split in 2
when i think of you
cause i know my path
is a life from you

i'm split in 3
you don't see me
you see the version i was
so we could never be

i'm split in 4
there's a door
to a world where i adore
you

i'm split in 5
i can't arrive
at a place where i'm alive
and well
i'm split in 6
koolaid mix
stones and sticks
in a cell
i'm split in 7
or maybe 11
maybe one of those mes'
creates a heaven

170

Split

i'm split in 2
when i think of you
cause i knew my path
is a life from you

i'm split in 3
you don't see me
you see the version i was
so we could never be

i'm split in 4
there's a door
to a world where i adore
you

i'm split in 5
i can't arrive
at a place where i'm alive
and well
i'm split in 6
koolaid mix
stones & sticks
in a cell
i'm split in 7
or maybe 11
maybe one of those me's'
~~goes up to heaven~~
creates a heaven

171

SELF-DECONSTRUCTED

there's self-deconstruction on your lips
sold like lemonade with saran wrap
black creased dickies running with chucks
talking more with each concrete toe tap

the white tee that's too large for my
torso has torn at the seams it seems
hooping is how we let off steam
we dream in dialects accented
we scream in 1s and 0s
to hackers

chipped on the ankle bone trackers
touched by taser ultraviolet lasers
bloody razors that kissed a pulse
of people too beat
to let their heartbeat any longer

does living make you stronger?
or weaker?
are we all just drug seekers?
synthesized from drug beakers?

172

SELF-DECONSTRUCTED

there's self-deconstruction on your lips
sold like lemonade with saran wrap
black creased dickies running with chucks
talking more with each concrete toe tap
change in time like a metronome
laying on the bed of a couple bucks

the white tee that's too large for my
torso has torn at the seams it seems
hooping is how we let off steam
we dream in dialetects accented
we scream in 1s and 0s
to hackers

chipped on the ankle bone trackers
touched by tasers ultraviolet lasers
bloody razors that kissed a pulse
of people too firebeat
to let their heartbeat any longer

does living make you stronger?
or weaker?
are we all just drug seekers?
synthesized from drug beakers?

173

DAISES ON MY ALTAR

i kept the daises that you conjured into a necklace
they sit dried amongst my altar
i give my emotions rude and reckless
as love begins to falter

i can't help but feel forgotten
you spit me out rude and rotten as
my apple core composted below the sink
my mind mirrors channel orange news
it's citrus when i think

you struck me like a cue ball
or like lightning
i could fight back
that thought is frightening
senses heightening
body tightening
body ripening
cue ball split
corner pocket
dislocate my shoulder socket

abusing my frame like an object
you love the power
sweet or sour
you coward

DAISES ON MY ALTAR

i kept the daises that you conjured into a necklace
they sit dried amongst my altar
i give my emotions rude and reckless
as love begins to falter

i can't help but feel forgotten
you spit me out rude and rotten as
my apple core composted below the sink
my mind mirrors channel oarnge news
it's citrus when i think

you struck me like a cue ball
or like lightning
i could fight back
that thought is frightening
senses heightening
body tightening
body ripening
cue ball split
corner pocket
dislocate my shoulder socket

abusing my frame like an object
you love the power
sweet or sour
you coward

BRIDGE ASHES

after the bridge burned
it took me some time to find solace
for the loss of my sanctuary is one
to lament for a lifetime

recreating time and space is for the gods
and in that department i lack the delusion
for that complex the context is
this body is my vessel
and one day i will have no choice
but to depart — can i grow indifferent to this?

it feels that
the ebb and flow of my body's depression
has caused a ripple effect in this river of
interconnecting streams
themes that replay in dreams
disassociated from reality as we know it
obstructing my ability to be "here"

i thought i needed time, so much so that
i was obsessed on buying it, possessing it
thinking i could create a savings account of it
but life has had its own agenda
detached from my desire
so to the unknown i go
all i have is my fire

BRIDGE ASHES

after the bridge burned
it took me some time to find solace
for the loss of my sanctuary is one
to lament for a lifetime

recreating time and space is for the gods
and in that department i lack the delusion
for that complex the context is
this body is my vessel
and one day i will have no choice
but to depart — can i grow indifferent to this?

it feels that
the ebb and flow of my body's depression
has caused a ripple effect in this river of
interconnecting streams
themes that replay in dreams
disassociated from my reality as we know it
obstructing my ability to be "here"

i thought i needed time, so much so that
i was obsessed on buying it, possessing it
thinking i could create a savings account of it
but life has had its own agenda
detached from my desire
so to the unknown i go
all i have is my fire

XONOCHROMATIC

one would think that when a heart breaks so many times
it closes but i think the opposite actually occurs
if not for drunken slurs or worried weres'
i think it opens up in a way that is
inexpressible with the english tongue
a monochromatic feeling
the taste of the color the smell of spring
nostalgic of an impression that sings
of hope

you want a reason to live
to find meaning in this meaningless mania
the truth is. . . you have to create that answer for yourself
if you aren't circumstantially given one

an asymmetrical dichotomy
i didn't know that i could say no

reclaiming autonomy from
the hands below and eyes above

you make me feel more symmetrical than i am
my brittle bones like crackers
to be flexible as water
the reactor
retractor
the actor

178

XONOCHROMATIC

one would think that when a heart breaks so many times
it closes but i think the opposite actually occurs
if not for drunken slurs or worried weres'
i think it opens up in a way that is
inexpressible with the english tongue
a monochromatic feeling
the taste of color the smell of spring
nostalgic of an impression that sings
of hope

you want a reason to live
to find meaning in this meaningless mania
the truth is... you have to create that answer for yourself
if you aren't circumstantially given one

an asymmetrical dichotomy
i didn't know that i could say no

reclaiming autonomy from
the hands below and eyes above

you make me feel more symmetrical then i am
my brittle bones like crackers
to be flexible as water
the reactor
retractor
the actor

AKATHREADS

you are consistent in my inconsistent world
a nostalgic reminder of a life that i once craved
an idea of a person that i needed to abandon
in order to save myself

by chance

you came in the form of the love of my life
and left in the form of a friend
and although it's been years
i hope that i'll see you in the end
of a beginning

because you being alive is precious to me
and something that i cherish
more than memories
the burned bridge between us
reminds me how ashes can become nutrients

fear and shame
you knew my ego well
so much so that
i have lived with these shackles
bound in cell
we create our hell

Akathreads

you are consistent in my inconsistent world
a nostalgic reminder of a life i once craved
an idea of a person that i needed to abandon
in order to save myself

by chance

you came in the form of the love of my life
and left in the form of a friend
and although its been years
i hope that i'll see you in the end
of a beginning

because you being alive is precious to me
and something that i cherish
more than memories
the burned bridge between us
reminds me how ashes can become nutrients

fear and shame
you knew my ego well
so much so that
i have lived with those shackles
bound in cell
we create our hell

CONDUIT

with ancient conversations approached humbly
we found ourselves in a discussion with decision
on how life and death in a tongue
requires precision

what a fleeting feeling of flight
the bird caged from light
the lower you feel the higher the height
and the darker you see the brighter the light

we're bound like books
that tend to miss someone's touch
when you hold my spine
you won't feel much but oxidized pages

we can't heal by ourselves if we were hurt by others
after a lifetime being in moribund
to life i said, "yes."
even if my inner child is in need of CPS
even if my waterfilled lungs are in need of CPR
if your pockets are like the mason jars
then mine are like swimming pools
silver tongue gold teeth skimming fools
jewels of knowledge
the power to acknowledge
my own ignorance

CONDUIT

with ancient conversations approached humbly
we found ourselves in a discussion with decision
on how life and death in a tongue
requires precision

what a fleeting feeling of flight
the bird caged from light
the lower you feel the higher the height
and the darker you see the brighter the light

we're bound like books
that tend to miss someone's touch
when you hold my spine
you ~~witch~~ won't feel much but oxidized pages

we can't heal by ourselves if we were hurt by others
after a lifetime of being in ~~the doorway of~~ moribund
to life i said "yes"
even if my innerchild is in need of cps
even if my waterfilled lungs are in need of cpr
if your pockets are like mason jars
then mine are like swimming pools
silver tongue gold teeth skimming fuels
jewels of knowledge
the power to acknowledge
my own ignorance

CRAVING

don't you crave to be nurtured
to be held when you don't feel whole?
i know i do

juxtaposed jumpers
like the kissing of car bumpers in city streets
emotional alchemy meets searching for potions
nectar needed in the neediest of notions
grab the jab of a boxer in their prime
amazon the packaged crime
what an elixir of life

with the eyes of a storm
and a sting of a swarm
deviation from norm
mask off deform

parasitic by circumstance
and loving by nature
a dichotomy that
needs semblance

CRAVING

don't you crave to be nurtured
to be held when you don't feel whole?
i know i do

juxtaposed jumpers
like the kissing of car bumpers in city streets
emotional alchemy meets searching for potions
nectar needed in the neediest of notions
grab the jab of a boxer in their prime
amazon the packaged crime
what an elixir of life

with the eyes of a storm
and a sting of a swarm
deviation from norm
mask off deform

parastic by circumstance
and loving by nature
a dichotomy that
needs semblance

SANCTUARY

tending trust that has been broken into fragments
stale stagnant sour frantic feelings kiss the air
of frisco rooftops with deep despair

to miss a feeling never forged
in the echo of a thought lost in storage
the hissing mouth like the gas coming from the stove
thick rooted weeds in this garden's grove

show your radiance even in the darkness
but know that you will be othered in this process
it is the way of the land to create separation
the accepted and the outcast
you are built to outlast
desperation

the need to rejoice in a space of confusion
just be sure to dilute your delusion
because what can be held can be taken
fruit tree shaken
so hold your flame inside of you
where no hands can grasp and no ears
can hear
only here
will you find solace
protect this place because it will become
your sanctuary

SANCTUARY ⊕

tending trust that has been broken into fragments
stale stagnant sour frantic feelings kiss the air
of frisco rooftops with deep despair

to miss a feeling never forged
in the echo of a thought lost in storage
the hissing mouth like the gas coming from the stove
thick rooted weeds in this garden's grove

show your radiance even in the darkness
but know that you will be othered in this process
it is the way of the land to create separation
the accepted and the outcast
you are built to outlast
desperation

the need to rejoice in a space of confusion
just be sure to dilute your delusion
because what can be held can be taken
fruit tree shaken
so hold your flame inside of you
where no hands can grasp and no ears
can hear
only here
will you find solace
protect this place because it will become
your sanctuary

187

TIME

time has been
commodified just like me
circles for centuries
an ancient wisdom sought to sow
the more you learn the less you know

i am bound to grow, stagnate, or die
my attitude to what happened is up to me
acceptance surrender survival
change is the only constant
spiritual revival

submit to suffering
and what she has to teach
self-love will only take you so far
communion is reunion for my nervous system's beach
i jump in the cold pacific to jolt myself back within my friends' reach

you have to constantly choose wellness
and release the attachment to being broken
especially if you've built an identity around it
it was useful for your survival
but now it's your prison

TIME

time has been
commodified just like me
circles for centuries
an ancient wisdom sought to sow
the more you learn the less you know

i am bound to grow, stagnate, or die
my attitude to what happened is up to me
acceptance surrender survival
change is the only constant
spiritual revival

submit to suffering
and what she has to teach
"self-love" will only take you so far
communion is reunion for my nervous system's beach
i jump in the cold pacific to jolt myself back within my friends' reach

you have to constantly choose wellness
and release the attachment to being broken
especially if you've built an identity around it
it was useful for your survival
but now it's your prison

189

SOULITUDE

the conversion of
lonliness to solitude
a tender place to rest my soul

i used to ache in this desolation
but now i need the separation
in order to remember the meaning of myself
a thought
a body
a vessel

dust settles as i wrestle with mold smears on bread
days where i was dead were
days where i was too afraid to
be different from
the identities
that i knew
i created

elated diamond dropped in jello
screaming hello
i sat by the creek
weeping with the water's creep
from a place inside my soul
that i expected to be barren
but surprisingly was abundant

SOULITUDE

the conversion of
lonliness to solitude
a tender place to rest my soul

i used to ache in this desolation
but now i need the seperation
in order to remember the meaning of myself
a thought
a body
a vessel

dust settles as i wrestle with mold smears on bread
days where i was dead were
days where i was too afraid to
be different from
the identities
that i knew
i created

elated diamond dropped in jello
screaming hello
i sat by the creek
weeping with the water's creep
from a place inside my soul
that i expected to be barren
but suprisingly was abundant

ZAPATOS

a soul from soles that saw the sol
be welcomed to a country with a treacherous toll
we sing over deserts of cactus
with syncopated strides
and just like the cactus our water hides
deep within with flaring spines
we walk we walk to sharing lines
the predators you see they set the signs
they set the rules they set the fines
too tired to care and too thirsty not to drink
the enemies ocean is spiked with ink
cuz next thing we know
our own bodies of water are converted to labor
all that sacrifice only to change a neighbor
next thing we know
we change our names
we change our clothes we change our aims
we send money back home but *home*
becomes a shadow of the past
an answer to a question when asked
where are you *really* from?

ZAPATOS

a soul from soles that saw the sol
be welcomed to a country with a treacherous toll
we sing over deserts of cactus
with syncopated strides
and just like the cactus our water hides
deep within with flaring spines
we walk we walk to sharing lines
the predators you see they set the signs
they set the rules they set the fines
too tired to care and too thirsty not to drink
the enemic's ocean that was once ours is spiked with ink
cuz next thing we know
we change our names
we change our clothes we change our aims
we send money back home but *home*
becomes a shadow of the past
an answer to a question when asked
where are you really from?

Room

there's a room
that's turning to a tomb
filled with loud silence
where dead flowers bloom

there's clothes scattered
cat litter on the floor
glass shattered
from too many dishes by the door

there's guitars with broken strings hanging on the wall
that collect specs
of dust
putrid is
the must
of depression
that even the sage bundle on my altar couldn't cleanse
smoke in a lens my favorite pen lost in laundry

there's this feeling only my eyes can tell
the yearning to shed this mortal shell
the longing to escape from this
moral cell
these feelings consume me
plague me
and slowly chip away at me
like the gray paint i hate

Room

there's a room
that's turning to a tomb
filled with loud silence
where dead flowers bloom

there's clothes scattered
cat litter on the floor
glass shattered
from too many dishes by the door

there's guitars with broken strings hanging on the wall
that collect specs
of dust
putrid is
the must
of depression
that even the sage bundle on my altar couldn't cleanse
smoke in a lens my favorite pen lost in laundry

there's this feeling only my eyes can tell
the yearning to shed this mortal shell
the longing to escape from this
moral cell
these feelings consume me
plague me
and slowly chip away at me
like the gray paint i hate

Mattress

cobalt locks on brass doors
my body is an afterthought on trashed floors
these four walls remind me what it is i'm for all fours
i try to talk back but my throat is dry and my lips are cracked
as a desert in summer cheeks smacked and bruised
used and abused until my skin turns into sunset hues in California.
this is a place not of rest or of prayer or of conversion
this is a place to forget forfeit submit surrender your versions.
how godless these surroundings are around my surrounding scars of
burns that remember what my mind can't. i see an ant
in the cracks of the drywall that
follows the snake path to the rotting apple core.
my clothes are stained and clumped
where a roach scurries over ashes dumped.
tracks of sediments of soil from a gargoyle
chainsmoker gasping for a breath of fresh air
the window hasn't been cracked in weeks
the pipes between the 2 by 4s swell and creeks.
he speaks
with bobwire gums and protruding ivory fangs
sinking those edges 8 inches below her bangs
the warmth of words goes cold quickly in this room
that smells like her moans of hormones and jasmine perfume.
bulk pickup has not allowed me an embrace
so i hide away with my mutilated face.
would you still witness me?

196

MATTRESS

cobalt locks on brass doors
my body is an afterthought on trashed floors
these four walls remind me what it is i'm for all fours
i try to talk back but my throat is dry and my lips are cracked
as a desert in summer cheeks smacked and bruised
used and abused until my skin turns into sunset hues in California.
this is a place not of rest or of prayer or of conversion
this is a place to forget forfeit submit surrender your versions.
how godless these surroundings are around my surrounding scars of
burns that remember what my mind can't. i see an ant
in the cracks of the drywall that
follows the snake path to the rotting apple core.
my clothes are stained and clumped
where a roach scurries over ashes dumped.
tracks of sediments of soil from a gargoyle
chainsmoker gasping for a breath of fresh air.
the window hasn't been cracked in weeks
the pipes between the 2 by 4s' swell and creaks.
he speaks
with bobwire gums and protruding ivory fangs
sinking those edges 8 inches below her bangs
the warmth of words goes cold quickly in this room
that smells like her moans of hormones and jasmine perfume.
bulk pickup has not allowed me an embrace
so i hide away with my mutilated face.
would you still witness me?

197

THE SOIL OF A GRAVE

it is time to say goodbye to you
my beautiful lifelong friend
you have given me your secrets
from start until this end

there is no other with your
soul printed poise
you are my familiar
the stillness in noise

you are
a fragrance that reminds me of home
a laugh that reminds me of joy
and an embrace that takes me back
to when i was young and curious

i do not have much time
so i must make this quick
because soon i will make friends
with the crows and ticks

i hope you remember me when i
become the soil you trek in joaquin miller
and i hope you remember me when
you have found another filler

THE SOIL OF A GRAVE

IT IS TIME TO SAY GOODBYE TO YOU
MY BEAUTIFUL LIFELONG FRIEND
YOU HAVE GIVEN ME YOUR SECRETS
FROM START UNTIL THIS END

THERE IS NO OTHER WITH YOUR
SOUL PRINTED POISE
YOU ARE MY FAMILIAR
THE STILLNESS IN NOISE

YOU ARE
A FRAGRANCE THAT REMINDS ME OF HOME
A LAUGH THAT REMINDS ME OF JOY
AND AN EMBRACE THAT TAKES ME BACK
TO WHEN I WAS YOUNG AND CURIOUS

I DO NOT HAVE MUCH TIME
SO I MUST MAKE THIS QUICK
BECAUSE SOON I WILL MAKE FRIENDS
WITH THE CROWS AND TICKS

I HOPE YOU REMEMBER ME WHEN I
BECOME THE SOIL YOU TREK IN JOAQUIN MILLER
I HOPE YOU REMEMBER ME WHEN
YOU HAVE FOUND ANOTHER FILLER

FRACTALS

nothing is mine
water to wine—d up blind

i'm never behind
if i'm in the present

the edge of mortality
next to the sobering truth
a refreshing reality
a clovering youth

i am who i love
a skyscraper of skies
a land that cannot be owned
the wondering whys'

the seasons of my soul
a blistering cold
for years
i'm anywhere but here
breaking all the mirrors
staring at the reflections

there are millions of me

FRACTALS

nothing is mine
water to wine-d up blind

i'm never behind,
if i'm in the present

the edge of mortality
next to the sobering truth
a refreshing reality
a clovering youth

i am who i love
a skyscraper of skies
a land that cannot be owned
the wondering whys'

the seasons of my soul
a blistering cold
for years
i'm anywhere but here
breaking all the mirrors
staring at the reflections

there are millions of me

201

I Hope Your Garden Grows

to have the container
to give and to receive
a spiritual practice
to learn and to grieve

an ebb and flow
to die, grow, and weave
in the spring you will
bloom, blow, and leave

seeking what you sought
bringing what you brought
thinking what you thought
only to see your cynical nature turn vapor
it's okay, give yourself the grace
you so kindly give others

your ego is your anchor
tied to this perception
a world dense in fluctuations
a paradoxical reflection
protection is particular to
those that need a worldly savior who
is the power of one
the power of none
the power of sun
the power of us

I Hope Your Garden Grows

to have the container
to give and to receive
a spiritual practice
to learn and to grieve

an ebb and flow
to die, grow, and weave
in the spring you will
bloom, blow, and leave

seeking what you sought
bringing what you brought
thinking what you thought
only to see your cynical nature turn vapor
it's okay, give yourself the grace
you kindly give others

your ego is your anchor
tied to this perception
a world dense in fluctuations
a paradoxical reflection
protection is particular to
those that need a worldly savior who
is the power of one
the power of none
the power of sun
the power of us

Afterglow

in the deepest of oceans
in the orbit of the sun
on the highest of mountains
there's nowhere left to run

i can't dissolve the borders
the borders between us all
sadly, i am no exception
i get no exemption
the rise is to the fall

these days
i feel shorter than my shadow
how it must feel to be taller than the redwoods
and warm as sunset hues that look like a nectarine bite
i don't wanna fight no more
i don't wanna be right no more
i wanna fly a kite some more
to reach into the sky
reaching for a meaning to carry me
and maybe
there is one
but most likely
there is none

there's no sure way to know
all i know is you look pretty in this after glow

AFTERGLOW

in the deepest of oceans
in the orbit of the sun
on the highest of mountains
there's nowhere left to run

i can't dissolve the borders
the borders between us all
sadly, i am no exception
i get no exemption
the rise is to the fall

these days
i feel shorter than my shadow
how it must feel to be taller than the redwoods
and warm as sunset hues that look like a nectarine bite
i don't wanna ~~no more~~ fight no more
i don't wanna be right no more
i wanna fly a kite some more
to reach into the sky
reaching for a meaning to carry me
and maybe
there is one
but most likely
there is none

there's no sure way to know
all i know is you look pretty in this afterglow

SUFFERING

suffering;
made me never want to cry again.
made me never want to try again.
made me want to get high again.
made me want to die again.

suffering while sober;
showed me the well of my tears.
showed me the flame of my spirit.
showed me the depth of my resolve.
it showed me the strength of my heart.

with time

suffering;
made me cry again.
made me start to try again.
suffering made me feel alive again
suffering brought me back to presence.

suffering while sober;
gave me the permission to hope again.
it gave me the permission to wait again.
it gave me the permission to pray again.
it gave me the permission to stay again.

SUFFERING

suffering;
made me never want to cry again.
made me never want to try again.
made me want to get high again.
made me want to die again.

suffering while sober;
showed me the well of my tears.
showed me the flame of my spirit.
showed me the depth of my resolve.
it showed me the strength of my heart.

with time

suffering;
made me cry again.
made me start to try again.
suffering made me feel alive again.
suffering brought me back to presence.

suffering while sober;
gave me the permission to hope again.
it gave me the permission to wait again.
it gave me the permission to pray again.
it gave me the permission to stay again.

How Much Does Grief Cost?

what do you do
when you don't have time for grief
when your days are filled with work and void of a relief

what do you do
when you're grieving an abuser
a conman a womanizer a victim blaming accuser
what do you do because it's time to clock in

what do you do
when you don't remember things as a kid
and your older sister has to remind you of all that he did
what do you do
when who you idolized turns out to be the villain
and then all of a sudden he ODs

what do you do
when you don't know what's true
when numbing the pain is all that he knew
so you understand

tell me what do you do
when you want to grieve this sober
but your car breaks down and you have to replace a motor
tell me what do you do because like my car
i try but i can't seem to start

<u>How Much Does Grief Cost?</u>

what do you do
when you don't have time for grief
when your days are filled with work and void of a relief

what do you do
when you're grieving an abuser
a conman a womanizer a victim blaming accuser
what do you do because it's time to clock in

what do you do
when you don't remember things as a kid
and your older sister has to remind you of all that he did
what do you do
when who you idolized turns out to be the villain
and then all of a sudden he ODs

what do you do
when you don't know what's true
when numbing the pain is all that he knew
so you understand

tell me what do you do
when you want to grieve this sober
but your car breaks down and you have to replace a motor
tell me what do you do because like my car
i try but i can't seem to start

Leave A Message At The

tone you left me with
there's a hugging corpse in the place
of where you used to be
your teeth are falling out
am i looking at me?
dream?

you nitpick me with memories like
the sores on your face
the aching of burdened bones
the shrinking of waist
requiem?

always broke as a promise
and always making more
my heart wants to believe you
death is a door.

i feel like you're always fighting cancer
but never want to answer
my calls
four black walls
with a mouth full of halls

cough drops to call drops to unanswered texts
chainsawed down family tree what did i expect?

LEAVE A MESSAGE AT THE

tone you left me with
there's a hugging corpse in the place
of where you used to be
your teeth are falling out
am i looking at me?
dream?

you nitpick me with memories like
the sores on your face
the aching of burdened bones
the shrinking of waist
requiem?

always broke as a promise
and always making more
my heart wants to believe you
death is a door.

i feel like you're always fighting cancer
but never want to answer
my calls
four black walls
with a mouth full of halls

cough drops to calls drops to unanswered texts
chainsawed down family tree what did i expect?

211

Fade

2 on top
0 on the sides
high and tight or a drop fade
but don't catch one
a dad or uncle's construction-working hands
jerking my head around to get rid of the line
strange how this is the only time
our head is touched by a father figure anymore
but intimacy is intimacy *right*?
even if it is a degree away from a fight
my scalp is white // the fade is just right

No Safety Net

moving house to house
while growing up
when i was sick they'd
always say i was faking it
never had dreams of making it
didn't feel like an option
that's how it is being poor
with sleep problems
no time to dream
no time to ruminate when
you don't have a room
elephants swept under the rug with a broken broom
kicked out more times then i can count. drinking to blackout
amounts. i can't recount. i can't recount.

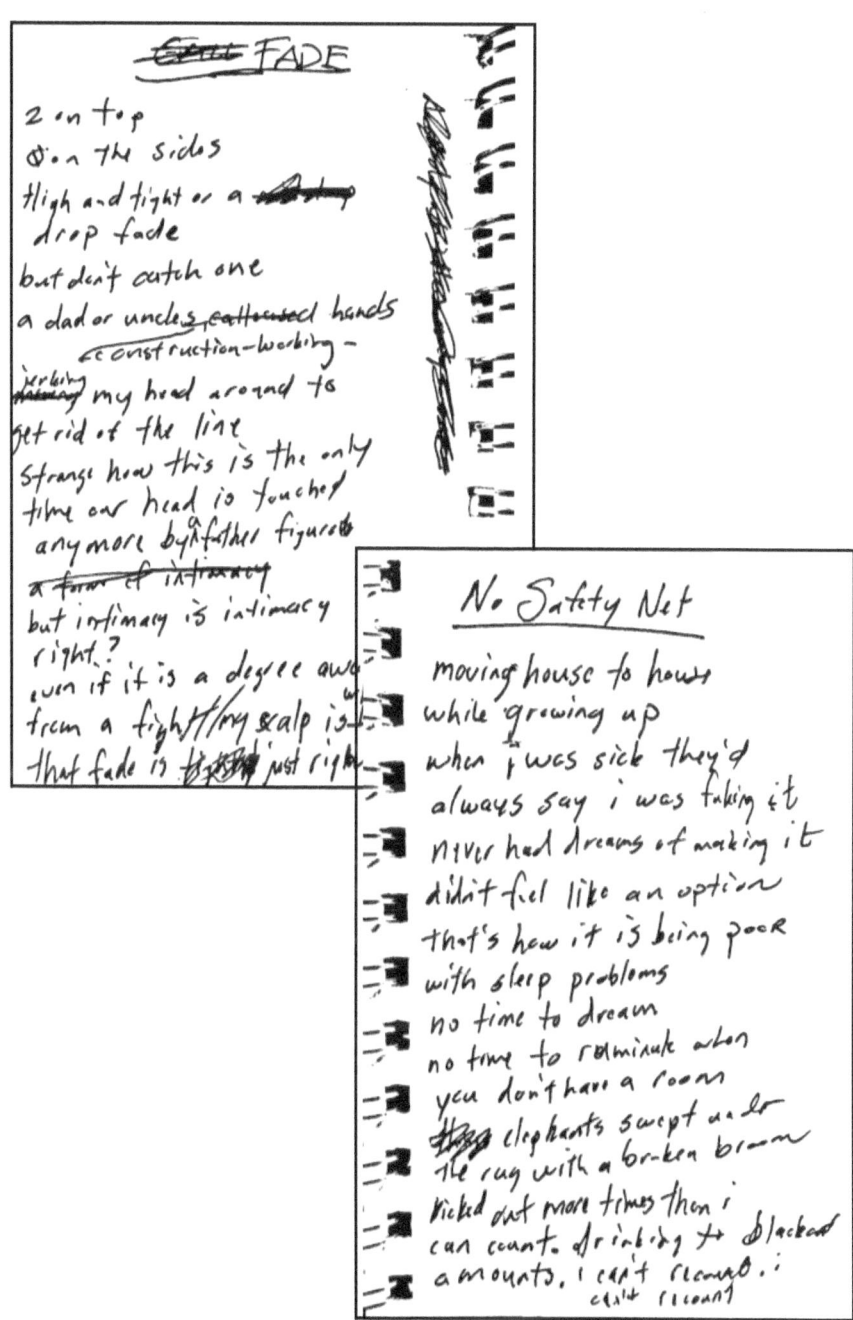

~~Still~~ FADE

2 on top
0 on the sides
High and tight or a ~~drop~~
drop fade
but don't catch one
a dad or uncle's ~~calloused~~ hands
~~construction-working~~ –
~~jerking~~ my head around to
get rid of the line
Strange how this is the only
time our head is touched
anymore by ~~a~~ father figures
~~a form of intimacy~~
but intimacy is intimacy
right?
even if it is a degree away
from a fight/my scalp is
that fade is ~~just right~~ just right

No Safety Net

moving house to house
while growing up
when i was sick they'd
always say i was faking it
never had dreams of making it
didn't feel like an option
that's how it is being poor
with sleep problems
no time to dream
no time to reminisce when
you don't have a room
~~they~~ elephants swept under
the rug with a broken broom
kicked out more times then i
can count, drinking to blackout
amounts, i can't recall..
~~can't recount~~

213

CHANGE

death is a door this is for
the lost versions of me
that i knowingly neglected
that i hid out of sight shamefully
that i tried to kill and bury in the backyard

death is a door this is for
the new versions of me that i haven't been before
the taking of responsibility, the holding of space, the (re)witnessing
the corrupted and distorted versions of myself

death is a door this is for
the ceasing of always wanting more
the processing of trauma
the re-telling of our stories
the reinvention of my inner dialogue
the transformation of suffering into art

death is a door this is for
the visitor i cannot ignore
the beginning of the journey
the start of an end

death is a door
this is for
you for me

CHANGE

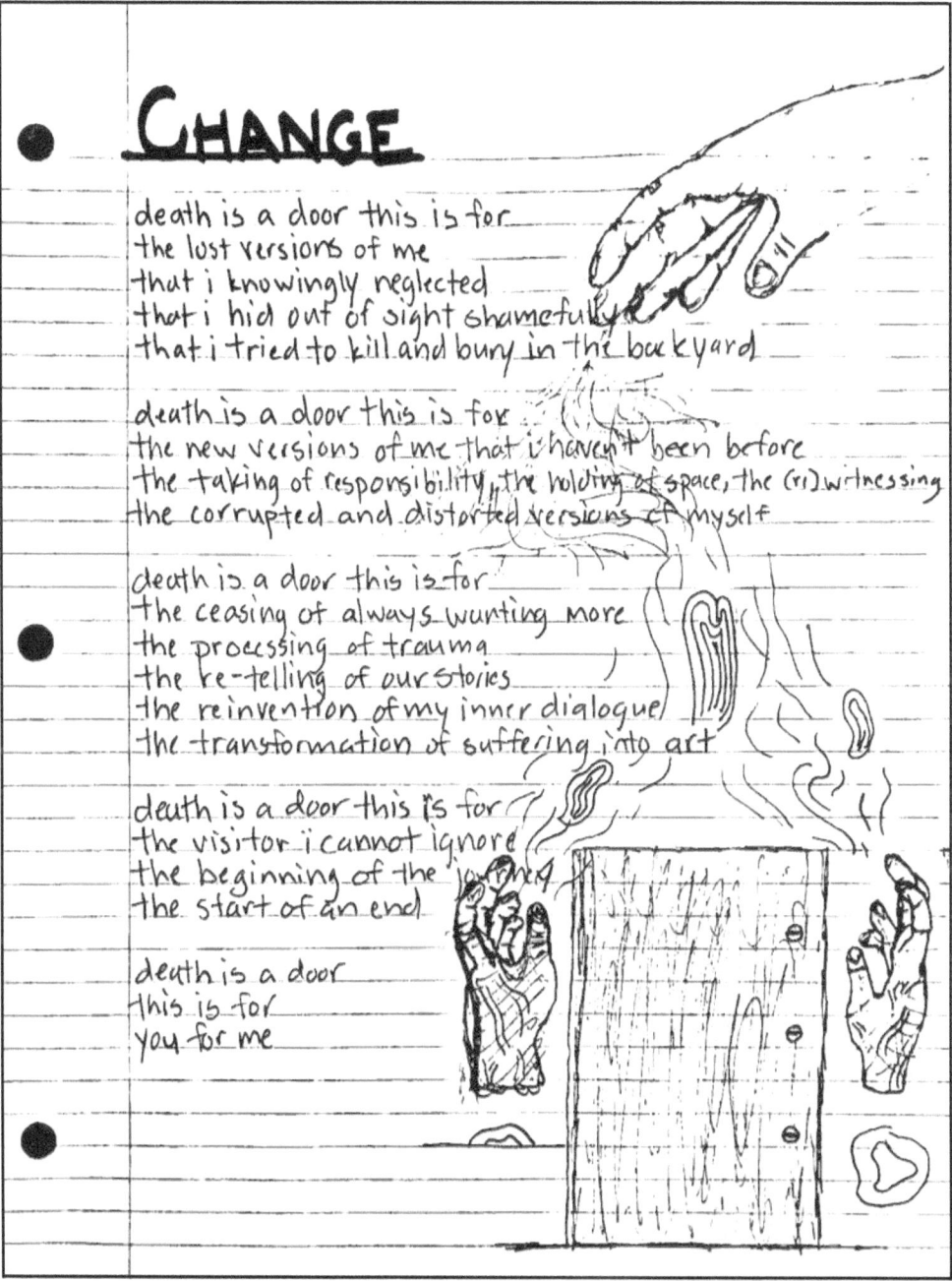

death is a door this is for
the lost versions of me
that i knowingly neglected
that i hid out of sight shamefully
that i tried to kill and bury in the backyard

death is a door this is for
the new versions of me that i haven't been before
the taking of responsibility, the holding of space, the (re)witnessing
the corrupted and distorted versions of myself

death is a door this is for
the ceasing of always wanting more
the processing of trauma
the re-telling of our stories
the reinvention of my inner dialogue
the transformation of suffering into art

death is a door this is for
the visitor i cannot ignore
the beginning of the journey
the start of an end

death is a door
this is for
you for me

VCR

the clouds roll by
for my cry to sky
the grief upon this heart
palpitates a sigh

you never knew why
and i didn't either
i was in survival mode when i hurt you
when i hurt me
i was hurting

but that doesn't excuse my actions does it?

even if wounds are weeping
apologies are seeping
chaos is creeping
stability for too long
is uncomfortable for me

time is catching up to me as i catch my breath
as my anxiety tries to settle and i'm processing death
in a linear way with non-linear feelings
time is passing and freezing
rewinding people pleasing
dilating and squeezing
the VCR stops when i press eject
it hurts when i reflect

VCR

the clouds roll by
for my cry to sky
the grief upon this heart
palpitates a sigh

you never knew why
and i didn't either
i was in survival mode when i hurt you
when i hurt me
i was hurting

but that doesn't excuse my actions does it?

even if wounds are weeping
apologies are seeping
chaos is creeping
stability for too long
is uncomfortable for me

time is catching up to me as i catch my breath
as my anxiety tries to settle and i'm processing death
in a linear way with non-linear feelings
time is passing and freezing
rewinding people pleasing
dialating and squeezing
the VCR stops when i press eject
it hurts when i reflect

GLOW GLANCE

emerald green river bed you shimmer
wondering thoughts that glimmer
in lips
small smooth rock skips
a light strum on your back to hips
grips
of water the right shade of blue
words like the wind in and through
grains of sand upon the hand
fall in crevices to understand
the mysteries of romance
where words slow dance
when eyes glow glance
luckily, we know chance

SUN DRUNK

sun drunk delirium and sun kissed
splashes of river water to some mist
on a body unflexed
i'm curious where touch goes next
hummingbirds butterflies dragonflies
in the stomach tattooed on thighs
playfully wrestling the skies in your eyes
that shapeshift from grey to kodak gold 200
tension in the air you could cut with a kiss
a love in abyss i got what i wanted
to let go or hold on to this?

GLOW GLANCE

emerald green river bed you shimmer
wondering thoughts that glimmer
in lips
small smooth rock skips
a light strum on your back to hips
grips
of water the right shade of blue
words like the wind in and through
grains of sand upon the hand
fall in crevices to understand
the mysteries of romance
where words slow dance
when eyes glow glance
luckily, we know chance

SUN DRUNK

sun drunk delirium and sun kissed
splashes of river water to some mist
on a body unflexed
i'm curious where touch goes next
hummingbirds butterflies dragonflies
in the stomach tattooed on thighs
playfully wrestling the skies in your eyes
that shapeshift from ~~gray~~ grey to kodak gold 200
tension in the air you could cut with a kiss
a love in abyss i got what is wanted
to let ~~go~~ go or hold on to this?

Hope 4 My Heart

my heart has lied before because it is a hoping heart
it would be untrue of me to say i wouldn't be hurt if we were to part
the slowness, the ease, the friendship of our start
and then
the way we looked at each other outside of bart
in your car
you pushed my hat down because my eyes went far
into your eyes where they swam the river
cold shivers on a sunny day with mangos and nectarines
playing songs of love and tangerines
the wind brought us together
and the water brought us even closer
mugwort, redwoods, and four leaf clovers
i think about that moment over and over
do you?

i was and am mesmerized
that this heart could hope this way again
i have your eyes memorized
i could sketch them with a pen
i adore you when i look at you
i'm in awe
of your movements in song, laugh, dance, and raw
form
you transform when you perform
cold days turn warm

am i in love?

HOPE 4 MY ♡

my heart has lied before because it is a hoping heart
it would be untrue of me to say i wouldn't be hurt if we were to part
the slowness, the ease, the friendship of our start
and then
the way we looked at each other outside of bart
in your car
you pushed my hat down because my eyes went far
into your eyes where they swam the river
cold shivers on a sunny day with mangos and nectarines
playing songs of love and tangerines
the wind brought us together
and the water brought us even closer
mugwort, redwoods, and four leaf clovers
i think about that moment over and over
do you?

i was and am mesmerized
that this heart could hope this way again
i have your eyes memorized
i could sketch them with a pen
i adore you when i look at you
i'm in awe
of your movements in song, laugh, dance, and raw
form
you transform when you perform
cold days turn warm

am i in love?

221

WHERE YOU WATER

if i get too close
the magic fades
if i stay too far
it's dying blades

i know you too much
to put you on a pedestal
but i don't know you enough
to let go of my "what if"

i was really in love with you
and i thought it'd last
but being in love is a feeling
just a feeling for the past

warmth always
a mirage of blue
an unfinished story
i hope to find you

in another life

WHERE YOU WATER

if i get too close
 the magic fades
if i stay too far
 its drying blades

i know you too much
 to put you on a pedestal
but i don't know you enough
 to let go of my "what if"

i was really in love with you
 and i thought it'd last
but being in love is a feeling
 just a feeling for the past

warmth always
 a mirage of blue
an unfinished story
 i hope to find you

in another life

SUMMER'S OVER

before the fingertip kissed the water
and the ripples didn't expand
before the knowing of names
before i felt your hand

maybe there was a chance
i'd find you at the lake
by that pond in the labyrinth of
the garden where
time is on a break

i'd call you by your name
give you something out of clay
to show you my hands know yours
and we'd sit and talk all day

we'd be the ones to make that swing
the ones that make blue
with you
i feel ease
if you're the ocean i'm the river
turn the deserts into seas

but maybe i'm just a romantic?
in love with what can never be
maybe love is safer in my mind
because only i can see

or maybe
i wish i found you before i found me
when life was much less bounding
i don't know how any of this is sounding
but i mean to say i love

SUMMER'S OVER

before the fingertip kissed the water
and the ripples didn't expand
before the knowing of names
before i felt your hand

maybe there was a chance
i'd find you at the lake
by that pond in the labyrinth of
the garden where
time is on a break

i'd call you by your name
give you something out of clay
to show you my hands know yours
and we'd sit and talk all day

we'd be the ones to make that swing
the ones that make blue
with you
i feel ease
if you're the ocean i'm the river
turn the deserts into seas

but maybe i'm just a romantic?
in love with what can never be
maybe love is safer in my mind
because only i can see

or maybe
i wish ~~you~~ i found you before you found me
when life was much less bounding
i don't know how any of this is sounding
but i mean to say i love

NON-LINEAR

again, i am humbled
i had to sell my 95' honda accord for
low rent that i could barely afford

3 months of a depression episode got me
into 3 seasons of debt
this feels like regression
but my medi-cal therapist says that
this is progression?

yeah, i guess running to catch the bus at 6:03
as the sun slowly rises and can't find me
is progress? i'm trying to find a love
in this process. but it's hard
when you force feed yourself chard
and have lived life always on guard

what was i expecting
to be secure in my 20s? funny.
i feel more alive now than all the times i had money.
the examined life is never pure.
the wise mind is never sure.
there's passion in this pain, right?
beauty in the struggle, before daylight??
maybe it's coming soon.
i really hope it is because all i feel
is pain being more present.

NON-LINEAR

again, i am humbled
i had to sell my 95' honda accord for
low rent that i could barely afford

3 months of a depression episode got me
into 3 ~~seasons~~ of debt
this feels like regression
but my medi-cal therapist says that
this is progression?

yeah, i guess running to catch the bus at 6:03
as the sun slowly rises and can't find me
is progress? im trying to find a love
in this process. but it's hard
when you force feed yourself chard
and have lived life always on guard

what was i expecting
to be secure in my 20s? funny.
i feel more alive now than all the times i had money.
the examined life is never pure.
the wise mind is never sure.
there's passion in this pain, right?
beauty in the struggle, before daylight??
maybe it's coming soon.
i really hope it is because all i feel
is pain being more present.

227

Notes To Self

i know that when the tears feel good on your face that
it's a good sign that you're healing.

i know that when you lose someone you find another
part of yourself that you either forgot or didn't know about.

i know that insecure people taught me that love was selfish
and that secure people showed me that love is like river water.

i know that people have abandoned me because they
were abandoned too.

i know that i mistook wanting to kill myself for not wanting
to feel the pain anymore. (an important distinction)

i know that if you know of a better way that
you typically choose that way.

i know, or at least i hope, that we are all loved by someone.

i know that eating a home-cooked meal with loved ones
tastes better than that same meal by myself.

i know that time is more valuable than money
because "money comes and goes" but time just goes.

NOTES TO SELF

i know when the tears feel good on your face that it's a good sign that you're healing.

i know that when you lose someone you find another part of yourself that you either forgot or didn't know about.

i know that insecure people taught me love was selfish and that secure people showed me that love is like river water.

i know that people have abandoned me because they were abandoned too.

i know that i mistook wanting to kill myself for not wanting to feel the pain anymore. (an important distinction)

i know that if you know of a better way that you typically choose that way.

i know, or at least i hope, that we are all loved by someone.

i know that eating a home-cooked meal with loved ones tastes better than the same meal by myself.

i know that time is more valuable than money because "money comes and goes" but time just goes.

I Want To Die

i want to die with golden hour filling my room. i want to feel the sun on my face one last time.

i want to die in my bed with covers over my legs particularly my feet cause they get cold. i know they'd appreciate that.

i want to die with my chosen family around me. i want them to tell me stories of our time together. i want us to laugh, to cry, to hug.

i want to die with my sense of humor because laughing has been my medicine. a few more jokes before i go.

i want to die knowing that i lived the kind of life that i could be proud of. i want to know that i tried my best to live.

i want to die after eating a meal with everyone i love and then drink one last cup of coffee in my favorite mug.

i want die with my hand being held as i go.

i want to die knowing that i told everyone bye and that i'll always be with them in some way.

i want to die knowing all the funeral expenses are paid for. i want to die, be cremated, and planted with the rootball of a tree. and lastly, i want to have permission to leave. i want to know that it's okay for me to go because i want peace to be the last feeling i have.

i WANT TO DIE

i want to die with golden hour filling my room. i want to feel the sun on my face one last time.

i want to die in my bed with covers over my legs particularly my feet cause they get cold. i know they'd appreciate that.

i want to die with my chosen family around me. i want them to tell me stories of our time together. i want us to laugh, to cry, to hug.

i want to die with my sense of humor because laughing has been my medicine. a few more jokes before i go.

i want to die knowing that i lived the kind of life i could be proud of. i want to know that i tried my best to live.

i want to die after eating a meal with everyone i love and then drink one last cup of coffee in my favorite mug.

i want to die with my hand being held as i go.

i want to die knowing that i told everyone goodbye and that i'll always be with them in some way.

i want to die knowing all the funeral expenses are paid for. i want to die, be cremated, and planted with the rootball of a tree. and lastly, i want to have permission to leave. i want to know that it's okay for me to go because i want peace to be the last feeling i have.

inspired by : Why Thinking About Death Helps You Live a Better Life / Alua Arthur
also inspired by : the Death & Dying course i took where we were asked to write out our deathbed scene

231

thank you for reading

special acknowledgments

thank you Jonny for that moment in the truck when you told me that i was wasting my potential as a person, i needed to hear that.

thank you Jess for the walks, the talks, the hot tea, the shared meals, and for being my friend through everything.

thank you Cele for the care, the love, and the check-ins.

thank you Tim for always believing in me and all my dreams. you've been there and supported all the artistic versions of me. you bought the first and maybe the only sold copy of my first poetry collection and it meant (and still means) the world to me.

thank you Zainab for all the books and time shared. the Saul & Aja book changed my poetry. and the Baldwin talk made me understand my responsibility as a poet in this world.

thank you Cara for the shared meals, the *Martyr* novel, putting me onto Hanif's work, as well as the times we doodled and hung out.

thank you Fin for that talk about editing, it was extremely helpful!

thank you Mom for doing the best you could with raising me. i wouldn't be where i am today without you. i love you.

thank you Sister for always checking on me. the calls mean so much to me. i'm proud of you, i'm proud of us.

and thank you Dad for the lessons that came before, during, and after you passed. may you rest in peace.

acknowledgments

thank you,

to everyone that has witnessed and walked with me along this journey. i have never achieved anything alone nor will i ever. to the authors, poets, musicians, prayers, friends, family, romances, and voices that inspired me, held me together, and showed me the path to keep going, i thank you. the depth of my gratitude is yours. and reader — thank you for spending your valuable time with me. i used all the resources at my disposal to be sure i honored our time together.

this collection was written over the course of many years and took all the stamina and mental fortitude that i could summon. the work required honesty, intuition, instinct, faith, surrender, clarity, delusion, patience, detachment, attachment, and most of all hope.

so i hope that this finds those that need it. i hope that this inspires others like the poets that inspired me. and i hope that by witnessing myself i was able to witness others.

- rigo

ALSO BY RIGO:

Youniverse

"A vulnerable collection of poetry & prose that uncovers the internal struggles of identity, depression, heartbreak, and healing. Divided into five chapters with accented sketches, *Youniverse* explores loss to love, abandonment to self-discovery, and the grief in displacement. readers find themselves immersed in a deeply intimate experience that explores a never before seen universe. "

some books read while writing

My Mother Was a Freedom Fighter by Aja Monet

There There by Tommy Orange

The Dead Emcee Scrolls by Saul Williams

The Teachings of Don Juan & Journey To Ixltan
by Carlos Castaneda

Between The World And Me by Ta-Nehisi Coates

The Power of One by Bryce Courtenay

Are Prisons Obsolete by Angela Davis

The Fire Next Time by James Baldwin

The Body Keeps Score by Bessel Van Der Kolk

Citizen Illegal by José Olivarez

Nejma & Salt by Nayyirah Waheed

All About Love by Bell Hooks

The Count of Monte Cristo by Alexandre Dumas

The Creative Act by Rick Rubin

Illusions & Jonathan Livingston Seagull
by Richard Bach

The Count Of Monte Cristo by Alexandre Dumas

The Prophet by Kahlil Gibran

There's Always This Year: On Basketball and Ascension
by Hanif Abdurraqib

Martyr! A Novel by Kaveh Akbar

www.ingramcontent.com/pod-product-compliance
Lightning Source LLC
Chambersburg PA
CBHW030917120626
46554CB00001B/179